SOCIAL ENTREPRENEURSHIP
WHAT EVERYONE NEEDS TO KNOW

SOCIAL ENTREPRENEURSHIP

WHAT EVERYONE NEEDS TO KNOW

DAVID BORNSTEIN AND SUSAN DAVIS

OXFORD
UNIVERSITY PRESS

2010

OXFORD
UNIVERSITY PRESS

Oxford University Press, Inc., publishes works that further
Oxford University's objective of excellence
in research, scholarship, and education.

Oxford   New York
Auckland   Cape Town   Dar es Salaam   Hong Kong   Karachi
Kuala Lumpur   Madrid   Melbourne   Mexico City   Nairobi
New Delhi   Shanghai   Taipei   Toronto

With offices in
Argentina   Austria   Brazil   Chile   Czech Republic   France   Greece
Guatemala   Hungary   Italy   Japan   Poland   Portugal   Singapore
South Korea   Switzerland   Thailand   Turkey   Ukraine   Vietnam

Copyright © 2010 by David Bornstein and Susan Davis

Published by Oxford University Press, Inc.
198 Madison Avenue, New York, New York 10016

www.oup.com

Oxford is a registered trademark of Oxford University Press.

Library of Congress Cataloging-in-Publication Data
Bornstein, David.
Social entrepreneurship : what everyone needs
to know / David Bornstein and Susan Davis.
p.   cm.
Includes bibliographical references.
ISBN 978-0-19-539634-8; 978-0-19-539633-1 (pbk.)
1. Social entrepreneurship.   2. Social change.
I. Davis, Susan.   II. Title.
HD60.B67 2010
361.7'65—dc22   2009044194

Printed in the United States of America
on acid-free paper

For Dad
—DB

For the changemaker in each of us
—SD

A single event can awaken within us a stranger
totally unknown to us.
To live is to be slowly born.
—Antoine de Saint-Exupéry

CONTENTS

ACKNOWLEDGMENTS

This book offers a short, general introduction to social entrepreneurship. The subject spans so much activity today that no small book can adequately cover it. But we have tried here to address a broad range of questions and point the way for further exploration. The result reflects our biases, which include shared exposures to the field of microfinance in Bangladesh and to the work of Ashoka and hundreds of social entrepreneurs in its fellowship. From our vantage point, they have exerted a dominant influence on the global field of social entrepreneurship. Others may place emphasis elsewhere.

We are grateful to Dayne Poshusta and Timothy Bent of Oxford University Press, who *insisted* that this book get written and provided thoughtful editorial guidance at every step of the way, and to Mildred Marmur, our literary agent, for her counsel and friendship. We are especially grateful to David's grandaunt Selma Arnold, 95, a language lover, who carefully read through this manuscript twice (even while in the hospital) and offered suggestions and corrections that improved almost every paragraph.

—DB & SD

I would like to extend heartfelt thanks to the Skoll Foundation, William James Foundation and the Kellner Foundation, whose support made it possible for me to write this book, and to Civic Ventures, which served as my fiscal sponsor. Manuel Rosaldo and Emily Spivack, my colleagues at Dowser Media, offered thoughts and suggestions on a daily basis. Dean Furbush helped to clarify an important idea at the beginning of the book. Many other friends offered feedback and encouragement. I feel privileged to have met so many generous teachers and friends through my writing work, none wiser than my co-author, Susan, who has a special place in my heart. While I was working on this book, my mother progressed into advanced Alzheimer's disease. Living in another city, I don't think I would have been able to concentrate much on writing if not for the help I knew my parents could count on daily from my sister Lisa, brother Garner, and brother-in-law Steve, and from kind caregivers Carol and Jennifer. Whenever I called home, my father would pick up the phone and, no matter how his day had gone, would say, "How's that book coming along? I can't wait to read it." Those words were the biggest help. To Elijah, your inquisitiveness and playfulness, your love of Bengal tigers, golden eagles, and the Beatles, bring pure joy to life. And to Abigail, what can I say? You floor me. Je t'adore.

—DB

I would like to thank the many incredible social entrepreneurs around the world who I have been privileged to know over the years, as well as my colleagues at Ashoka, BRAC, Grameen, and NYU, from whom I have learned so much. You changed my world. I thank the many students, interns, and volunteers who inspire and teach me as they give me an opportunity to share my experience. My deepest appreciation is offered to my co-author and dear friend, David, whom I greatly admire and love. He insisted that I collaborate with him on this book. What a gift it turned out to be—complete with beautiful dinners with Abigail and Elijah! I also thank my family and friends who put up with me, encouraged, and supported me during this process. You know who you are.

—SD

A NOTE ON TERMS

No field of work should be defined in the negative. Accordingly, we have tried to avoid relying on terms like "nonprofit" and "nongovernmental organization" (NGO). We refer more often to "social," "social-purpose," and "citizen-sector organizations," and the term "social entrepreneur" when referring to founders of organizations that exhibit the qualities described in the book. "Social enterprise" denotes an organization that attacks problems through a business format, even if it is not legally structured as a profit-seeking entity. An "intrapreneur" drives positive change within an existing organization or business. And a "changemaker" advances change in myriad ways beyond the roles outlined above.

INTRODUCTION

For much of the past decade, the specter of 9/11 has hovered like a dark cloud, a stark reminder that we have entered a phase of human history in which individuals can destabilize nations. The global dispersion of information, technology, and organizing capability has forced governments to rethink the basis of human security. These forces have also caused many to rethink the way we address global problems. Just as individuals and small groups have more destructive capability now, they also have more *constructive* capability.

This is fortuitous because the need for change is urgent. The United Nations recently reported that one billion people face hunger as a result of the financial crisis. Millions of women and girls die prematurely due to violence or the denial of medical care. Deadly diseases circulate globally with astonishing speed. Coral reefs are being destroyed, species are going extinct, fresh water reserves are being depleted, global warming is accelerating. At home we struggle to fix health care and financial systems that have run dangerously out of control.

Many respond to the onslaught of problems by tuning out the world, getting lost in distractions, or adopting an attitude of cynical detachment. Many would like to take action but feel overwhelmed, don't know where to begin, or feel that problems are too big to be solved. But many have also found ways to respond with creativity, energy, and even optimism—attacking global, national, and local problems with powerful ideas and new tools. They see problems that are being ignored or mishandled by traditional institutions. In addition to registering protest, they are building new solutions.

Their stories have gone underreported. Even as news and information inundate us, the proliferation of people building new organizations to address social problems—millions of them—remains largely hidden from view. We know far more about the world's problems than about the world's problem *solvers*. This book draws attention to their efforts.

We refer to the landscape of organizations described above as the "citizen sector"; we believe that "social entrepreneurship" represents its leading edge. The book summarizes some of the historical underpinnings of this global phenomenon and suggests implications for the future. It asks the question that today's legion of changemakers are attempting to answer: how can people adapt rapidly, on an ongoing basis, to an ever-changing array of unforeseeable and increasingly critical problems?

Because of the size of the global population, the pace of change, the spread of technology, the urgency of financial, health, and environmental crises, and the interdependence that has collapsed boundaries, our response time must quicken: we must anticipate problems and attack them at their sources before they grow and multiply. And we must continually invent new solutions as conditions change.

The emergence of the citizen sector and social entrepreneurship are an adaption to the changing demands of the global environment, a departure from the top-down, centralized problem-solving model that dominated the past century. They favor an integrated, decentralized approach that harnesses the efforts of creative problem solvers far and wide.

Consider some developments from the past few decades. Microfinance organizations are expanding economic opportunities for hundreds of millions of poor people; rural schools and libraries deliver quality education to places beyond the reach of asphalt; health innovations release people from illness and prevent child deaths by expanding access to prenatal care, vaccines, micronutrients, and medicines; human rights advocates undermine the attitudes that cause exclusion based on race, gender, religion, sexual orientation, and disability; social businesses increasingly look to market products that meet basic human needs and reduce our environmental footprint; educators are developing methods that successfully teach empathy and conflict resolution skills; international networks have overcome nationalist forces to safeguard human rights at the global level.

Although problems are being attacked from many directions, today's changemakers share one common feature: they are building platforms that unleash human potential. They struggle to increase the number of people who have the opportunity to contribute their talents to the world. In so doing, they help more people to live with dignity.

It takes many kinds of actors to advance change: people who initiate new ideas and institutions (or renew old ones); a larger number who collaborate in building those institutions directly; and a much larger number who support those efforts in different ways. Over the past quarter century, the field of social entrepreneurship has gained a better understanding of the interplay among the roles. Describing the evolution of thinking like generations of the Worldwide Web would break it down as follows:

Social entrepreneurship 1.0 involved a concerted effort to: (1) Systematically identify people with innovative ideas and practical models for achieving major societal impact; (2) Describe their function in society and shine a spotlight on their work; and (3) Develop support systems to help them achieve significant social impact.

Social entrepreneurship 2.0 shifted into the terrain of organizational excellence. It drew heavily on insights from business strategy, finance, and management and was primarily concerned with helping social entrepreneurs build sustainable, high impact organizations or enterprises. Many people with expertise in the business sector were attracted to the field during this phase as they discovered new avenues to apply their talents.

Social entrepreneurship 3.0 (today) looks beyond individual founders and institutions to the change-making potential of *all* people and their interactions. It recognizes that social entrepreneurship is contagious. Every person who starts a social change organization emboldens others to pursue *their* ideas and solutions, whether by building institutions or by strengthening existing solutions through their investing, philanthropy, managing, advocacy, research, teaching, policy making, computer programming, purchasing, writing, and so forth.

The field of social entrepreneurship is improvising its own ecosystem of supports by stimulating more changemaking as it grows. These developments are spontaneous; there is no single source of leadership, but, rather, countless responses to emerging needs. They are scattered around the globe. Individually many of the actions seem small, but they are interconnected and mutually reinforcing. Taken together, they add up to more than the sum of their parts.

They are like the ant colony described by Lewis Thomas 35 years ago in *The Lives of a Cell*:

> A solitary ant, afield, cannot be considered to have much of anything on his mind; indeed, with only a few neurons strung together by fibers, he can't be imagined to have a mind at all, much less a thought. He is more like a ganglion on legs. Four ants *together*, or ten, encircling a dead moth on a path, begin to look more like an idea. They fumble and shove, gradually moving the food toward the Hill, but as though by blind chance. It is only when you watch the dense mass of thousands of ants, crowded together around the Hill, blackening the ground, that you begin to see the whole beast, and now you observe it thinking, planning, calculating. It is an intelligence, a kind of live computer, with crawling bits for its wits.

While human foresight is also limited, we *do* have our own ideas. We can imagine, and sometimes even predict accurately, how our individual actions might contribute to a larger end, even if the long-term consequences are unknowable. We can create structures and platforms that coordinate, rationalize, and augment our diverse efforts. The examples of the International Campaign to Ban Landmines and the Microcredit Summit Campaign come to mind. Both successfully aligned the efforts of thousands of groups to achieve shared global goals.

Social entrepreneurship 3.0 is concerned with building platforms that enable more people at every age to think and behave like changemakers *and* to help them work together powerfully in teams and in teams of teams. It looks to forge stronger linkages across cultural and disciplinary boundaries, particularly with business and government, and facilitate the rapid circulation and sharing of solutions at the global level.

The study of social entrepreneurship sheds light on how change happens and how societies renew themselves. It can help explain why government and international aid efforts have often met with limited success or outright failure, and what needs to be done differently in order to achieve better results. It also adds a dimension to the study of democracy, expanding the role of the citizen beyond choosing government representatives. In the years ahead, we believe many more citizens will consider it natural to take the lead in the creation of solutions to social problems. A quarter century ago, it took unusual confidence and vision to become a social entrepreneur. The role was undefined; examples were rare. Today, the path is becoming clear.

There is no way of knowing whether the constructive forces will overcome the destructive ones. As Bill Clinton has observed: "We're in a race against the positive and negative implications of our interdependence." Despite the problems, our spirits rise when we consider the historical changes that have enabled millions to take concerted and coordinated action to solve problems. Our hope is that this book will spark your excitement, expand your sense of possibility, and perhaps point the way to your own changemaking path.

SOCIAL ENTREPRENEURSHIP

WHAT EVERYONE NEEDS TO KNOW

I

DEFINING SOCIAL ENTREPRENEURSHIP

What is social entrepreneurship?

Social entrepreneurship is a process by which citizens build or transform institutions to advance solutions to social problems, such as poverty, illness, illiteracy, environmental destruction, human rights abuses and corruption, in order to make life better for many. Academics, practitioners, and philanthropists characterize it variously as a profession, field, and movement. The most widely cited definition was offered by Greg Dees, who is often referred to as the father of social entrepreneurship education. Dees draws on the thinking of the economists Jean-Baptiste Say and Joseph A. Schumpeter, who argued that entrepreneurs improve the productive capacity of society and provide the "creative destruction" that propels economic change. Dees holds that social entrepreneurs do the same for social change, creating new combinations of people and resources that significantly improve society's capacity to address problems. Social entrepreneurs, he explains, create public value, pursue new opportunities, innovate and adapt, act boldly, leverage resources they don't control, and exhibit a strong sense of accountability.

Dees has identified two schools of thought in the United States that focus on enterprise development and innovation. The former emphasizes organizational strategy, revenue generation, and financial planning as centerpieces of high-impact enterprises, while the latter focuses on breakthrough insights. Some scholars hold to an inclusive definition that accommodates many forms of changemaking behavior; others use the term to characterize only those with uncommon creativity, courage, and tenacity whose work produces large-scale transformational change.

Despite the absence of a universally accepted definition, the term has proved useful because it builds on long-held understandings about entrepreneurs but applies them in new ways. By demonstrating how entrepreneurial qualities can be channeled to address major problems, it has opened up new pathways of behavior and methods of analysis for people who are motivated by a desire to solve those problems.

Social entrepreneurs have always existed. But in the past they were called visionaries, humanitarians, philanthropists, reformers, saints, or simply great leaders. Attention was paid to their courage, compassion, and vision but rarely to the practical aspects of their accomplishments. Thus, people may know about the moral teachings of St. Francis but not about how the Franciscans became the fastest growing religious order of its day. Children learn that Florence Nightingale ministered to wounded soldiers but not that she built the first professional school for nurses and revolutionized hospital construction. Gandhi is remembered for demonstrations of nonviolent resistance but not for building a decentralized political apparatus that enabled India to make a successful transition to self-rule. And everybody knows that Martin Luther King Jr. declared "I have a dream" on the steps of the Lincoln Memorial, but few know that Asa Philip Randolph and Bayard Rustin orchestrated the March on Washington and made sure that King could make the maximum impact by speaking last.

A careful reader of history could identify the hidden hand of social entrepreneurs in the creation of many institutions and movements that we take for granted. However, it wasn't until the seventeenth century that societies began to accelerate the broad structural reforms that would allow large numbers of people to become entrepreneurs. The changes began in Europe where, for centuries, the Crown monopolies, the Church, the feudal lords, and the guilds had restricted commercial activity, discouraged innovation, and tied people to land and parishes. Not only was there little scope for independent trade at any scale, but people had little freedom or incentive to use their enterprise. As Robert Heilbroner explains in *The Worldly Philosophers*, in seventeenth-century France button makers were arrested for experimenting with cloth, and thousands of merchants were sent to the galleys, broken on the wheel, and hanged simply because they imported printed calicoes for sale.

The forces that overturned the old way of life in Europe— population growth, urbanization, scientific advances, improvements in transportation, and accumulated wealth—compelled traditional structures to relinquish some control over social and commercial activity. During the Enlightenment, new religious and philosophical beliefs, particularly the advent of political liberalism and the theory of natural rights—the rights to "life, liberty and property" in John Locke's famous formulation—provided a moral and conceptual foundation for modern economics and democracy. These ideas helped demarcate a new sector of society—a private sector—in which individuals could reorganize the patterns of production in order to capture the benefits of their enterprise.

To make sense of the forces unleashed by these historic changes, the dismal science, economics, was born. Its founding text, *The Wealth of Nations* by Adam Smith, was published in 1776. This coincided with the birth of the United States, the nation that more than any other would place economic liberalism at the center of national discourse.

Historians have pointed to one event that occurred during the Renaissance as among the most significant in modern history: the creation of the limited-liability joint-stock corporation. This legal innovation made it possible and attractive for investors to pool capital to build companies that could grow virtually without limit. To get an idea of the implications, consider that in the United States today, although 99.7 percent of all companies have fewer than five hundred employees, the tiny percentage of firms above this mark employ almost half the nation's salaried workers.

Corporations have grown immensely powerful. Three hundred multinational corporations control roughly a quarter of the world's wealth. Their managers frequently make decisions that run counter to the long-term interests of the public and even their own shareholders, as the recent financial crisis has illustrated. Some view these derelictions as an unavoidable consequence of the corporate legal structure. For example, in his book *The Corporation*, law professor Joel Bakan argues that while a corporation enjoys the legal status of a person, it is free of the social and legal forces that ensure good behavior from real people, such as empathy, public disapproval, and the threat of imprisonment. "Unlike the human beings who inhabit it," he writes, "the corporation is singularly self-interested and unable to feel genuine concern for others in any context." (Today, many social entrepreneurs with backgrounds in law and finance are working to change rules and incentive structures to ensure greater social responsibility from corporations.)

As the business sector developed, institutions were constructed to accelerate the flow of capital, provide business and management training, reward firms for better performance, spread business knowledge throughout society, facilitate business start-ups, and, in some countries, regulate business and financial activities. These institutions and regulations include antitrust laws, stock exchanges, business schools, accounting firms, securities and exchange commissions, business journalism, and, in recent years, venture capital.

What was the effect of the emergence of business entrepreneurship? The economist William J. Baumol has noted that during the 1700s, per-capita incomes in Europe are estimated to have risen 20 or 30 percent; during the 1800s, they rose 200 to 300 percent. And during the 1900s, the conservative estimate is that per-capita income in free-market economies increased 700 percent.

The rise of modern business created new wealth (large middle classes), new comforts (washing machines, electric lights, faster transportation), new patterns of living (40-hour workweeks, vacation time, retirement), and many new problems, including population displacement, the decimation of traditional cultures, abusive labor practices, environmental disasters, and the exploitative pursuit of cheap minerals and energy sources—many of the causes of the maldevelopment that continues to haunt much of the world, from West Virginia to the Congo to Iraq.

The intimate relationship between the two forms of entrepreneurship is evident in the fact that many of the most familiar examples of social entrepreneurship in the United States came about in response to problems *created* by the successes of business and were financed by the philanthropy of industrialists and the pooled wages of their workers.

Consider the surge of creative citizen activity in the United States between 1880 and 1920, when the country was rapidly being transformed from a collection of small, self-sufficient farms and midsize cities into an industrialized consumer society. Millions of immigrants and rural Americans were flooding into cities that were stretched beyond capacity—a situation comparable in many respects to the massive rural-to-urban migration occurring across the developing world today.

The new city dwellers had to learn how to translate their numbers into political power so they could change the oppressive conditions in America's slums and factories. It was during this period, the Progressive Age, that enlightened philanthropists began experimenting with "scientific charity," which aimed to transform the conditions that produced poverty, not just to provide comfort to the poor and ease the consciences of the rich. This era produced many of the organizations that form the American tapestry: the Salvation Army, the Urban League, the Lions Clubs, the Boy and Girl Scouts, Goodwill Industries, the PTA, the NAACP, Hull House, Rotary International, the YWCA, the League of Women Voters, many labor unions, and hundreds of other such organizations.

The United States was unusual in the degree that its citizenry self-organized to address problems almost from the nation's inception. As far back as the 1830s, Alexis de Tocqueville wrote that Americans seemed to possess a unique propensity for creating associations. It is no longer clear that America is exceptional in this regard, given the explosion of social entrepreneurship today in places as diverse as Brazil, India, Thailand, and South Africa. What is clear is that Americans were the beneficiaries of laws and attitudes highly favorable to social entrepreneurship—laws that can be directly traced to England's Charitable Uses Act of 1601, which defined roles for citizens in the redressing of social problems. The U.S. Constitution stipulates that all powers not explicitly given to the states or to the federal government are given to the people. Both the presumption of a robust citizen domain and U.S. nonprofit law were departures from the global norm. Many countries would not put similar laws in place until the 1990s. In France, which was Tocqueville's reference point, private social service associations were banned until 1901.

The rush of citizen activity that Americans experienced a century ago when faced with a profound and painful transition is analogous to today's global changes.

When did it emerge as a global movement?

To answer this we need to consider the human condition in the past. In *Bury the Chains*, Adam Hochschild explains that at the end of the eighteenth century, well over three-quarters of all people were living in slavery or serfdom. Of those *not* enslaved, the majority were forced to submit to the rule of kings or dictators, locked into immutable traditions that did not permit dissent, or consigned to short lives characterized by crushing poverty, disease, and violence.

Until recently, even in developed countries, women, dark-skinned people, the disabled, and any number of minority groups were segregated, denied the vote, or subjected to additional forms of discrimination often backed up by the full weight of law. Members of these groups continue to face discrimination, while gay, lesbian, and transgender people are still struggling for equality under the law. Over the past forty years, however, social norms have evolved, and opportunities have opened up for many of them. Around the globe, the changes have been even more dramatic, as authoritarian governments have fallen, education, health care, and communications have been extended to hundreds of millions of families, and economic growth has produced large middle classes. The result has been an explosion of citizen activity, including the establishment of millions of new social-purpose organizations.

The biggest driver of change has been the women's movement, which shifted aspirations and expanded the scope of possibility for women in many societies (though certainly not all). In recent years, leaders like Ela Bhatt, founder of the Self-Employed Women's Association in India, and Nobel Peace Prize winner Wangari Maathai, founder of the Green Belt Movement in Kenya, have established new pathways for women in Asia and Africa. And other long-marginalized groups, such as Afro-Brazilians, the Roma in Hungary, and the Dalit (untouchables) in India, have benefited from an array of social justice movements.

Since the 1970s, the world has witnessed the collapse of many communist and authoritarian regimes. Citizens regularly challenge power and convention in countries where, thirty or forty years ago, they might have been "disappeared," "banned," or imprisoned for doing so. Prior to the 1980s or 1990s, social entrepreneurs would not have been tolerated in such countries as Argentina, Brazil, Chile, Hungary, Indonesia, Nigeria, Pakistan, Poland, Portugal, South Africa, Spain, Thailand, or Vietnam. Although they still face dangers in some of these countries, many nevertheless operate openly.

Mikhail Gorbachev said that the single biggest factor behind the demise of the Soviet Union was the Beatles.

Decades before the advent of the Internet, radio, television, and cassettes made it difficult to contain ideas within borders and suppress human aspirations. We have to stop to recall that not long ago, leaders like Vaclav Havel and Stephen Biko were imprisoned or murdered because of the power of their words. To be sure, suppression continues in countries such as China, Iran, Myanmar, and North Korea. However, the uprisings that followed the fraudulent Iranian election in 2009, chronicled globally via Twitter, demonstrated the problems governments now face in keeping citizens in the dark.

It was during the 1980s and 1990s that disparities in wealth and freedom grew particularly vivid to much of the world through global media. Governments and businesses found themselves closely scrutinized. With new exposures, people's expectations shifted. In many places, frustration and anger mounted about conditions (and abuses) that had previously gone unquestioned and unchallenged. Among global civil society organizations, a consensus emerged that governments too often failed in their core representative duties, and corporations too often exacerbated suffering and inequality and destroyed the environment for short-term gain. The clearest indication of the dissatisfaction with governments was the decline in voter turnout in virtually every nation where free elections were held. Governments, liberal and conservative alike, were widely perceived as impotent in the face of concentrated corporate power.

Governments conspicuously failed to stand up to business interests when it came to safeguarding the environment, protecting human rights, ensuring access to health care and decent working conditions, and regulating financial institutions. To many, it seemed that World Bank projects and IMF policies were explicitly designed to benefit the wealthy at the expense of the poor. Reforms were needed, and nowhere more than within the very institutions charged with protecting the public interest. But many recognized that change wasn't going to originate from within these institutions. For change to happen, new institutions and new spheres of power would need to be created.

This recognition coincided with the new freedoms described above and was supported by advances in education and health, which further strengthened the global citizenry. Between 1970 and 1985, adult literacy in the developing world increased from 43 to 60 percent. During the 1970s alone, the number of universities in the world doubled. During the twentieth century, largely owing to improvements in sanitation, the advent of antibiotics, and advances in plant genetics (which led to the Green Revolution), life expectancy soared from 25 to 63 in the developing world and from 45 to 75 in the developed world. Many other gains were concentrated over the past four decades. During the 1980s, for example, the global vaccination rate of children climbed from 20 percent to almost 80 percent, preventing millions of child deaths and disabilities annually.

Along with these changes came massive demographic shifts. The last decade of the twentieth century was the first in human history in which more people lived in cities than in the countryside. Two or three generations ago, the vast majority of the world's people still lived in villages or towns where communication with the outside world was limited. People tended to stay in one place all their lives and learned their work from their parents.

That world has disappeared, and, historically speaking, it vanished overnight. In a few decades, hundreds of millions fled villages and towns to find employment in cities. The urban population in developing countries was three hundred million in 1950. By 2025, it is expected to reach four and a half billion.

Urbanization intensifies economic change. Richard Florida, author of *The Rise of the Creative Class*, notes that the forty largest megaregions in the world—stretches of interconnected cities spanning hundreds of miles—are home to a fifth of the world's population but produce two-thirds of the world's economic output and 90 percent of its innovations. Urbanization has coincided with the growth of large middle classes in Brazil, China, India, Indonesia, and other developing countries. And because members of this class enjoy access to education, wealth, and political power yet remain less vested in historic systems of privilege, they often become highly effective social entrepreneurs.

Below the middle class, the expansion of economic opportunity has spread to tens of millions of families through microfinance and thousands of organization such as Kick-Start, TechnoServe, and International Development Enterprises, which provide assistance to small and medium-sized ventures. Increasingly, people in rural areas and slums possess the skills, resources, and confidence to create businesses and other organizations. Microfinance and business assistance often lead to higher levels of political engagement.

Along with these benefits, the headlong rural-to-urban migration of recent decades has imposed great hardships. Developing world cities—or megashantytowns—are often violent, unhealthy, and ugly, with people living amid open sewage and industrial pollution. Those who have been uprooted from the countryside due to forces beyond their control—a World Bank dam project, a multinational mining or logging company, or even a mortgage crisis that precipitates a worldwide recession—often feel adrift, anxious, and angry. Global warming is largely a result of consumption, industry, and farming in the West, but it is the poor in the developing world who will suffer most from the droughts, floods, and storms that scientists expect it to bring.

As the world has grown more urban and interdependent, the pace of change has accelerated. Today, our adaptive systems must keep pace. Whether it's the environmental threat, infectious diseases, global terrorism, or economic crises, we have little time to fix things when they go awry; nor can we address problems chiefly in a centralized manner. Solutions must be decentralized and integrated and deployed in real time.

Let's put it all together now. Large numbers of people around the world have experienced the removal of historic constraints. Attainment of their newfound freedoms coincides with more wealth, longer life spans, better communication, and an array of problems that necessitate the creation of new solutions.

Now consider what emerged over the past forty years: millions of new organizations aimed at addressing problems from every conceivable angle; and hundreds of new movements to protect the environment and the rights of consumers, eradicate landmines, expand access to microcredit, build and finance an array of social-purpose businesses, create an international criminal court, and protect the rights of people with disabilities, indigenous groups, gays and lesbians, and many others. People seeking solutions are no longer willing to wait for governments, corporations, churches, or universities to lead.

Historical changes have produced urgent and complex problems while simultaneously augmenting the capacity of people around the world to address those problems. What we are witnessing in the field of social entrepreneurship is the intersection of these forces as they unfold.

Who are the pioneers?

Even before the language of social entrepreneurship had been invented, it was clear that not all social purpose organizations—so-called nongovernmental or nonprofit organizations—performed equally well. Just as some businesses grow faster and are more profitable than others, some organizations achieve more social impact per dollar than others. And two groundbreaking examples of social entrepreneurship occurred in one of the poorest countries in the world: Bangladesh.

Bangladesh was born in 1971, in the wake of a massive cyclone and a war of independence that left the country in devastation. Up to five hundred thousand people died from the 1970 Bhola cyclone. During Bangladesh's war of independence, the Pakistani army raped hundreds of thousands of girls and women and murdered more than a million people. Cholera, typhoid, starvation, and other diseases claimed the lives of up to two million more. Ten million refugees fled to India.

The war and cyclone generated sympathy and outrage on a global scale. International development agencies converged on Dhaka, ready to provide aid. The conventional practice at the time was for development assistance to flow directly from governments of wealthy countries to governments of poor countries, and from the top to the bottom through local government channels. However, large amounts of free money will almost always produce corruption, and Bangladesh's nascent government—which included idealistic freedom fighters as well as political cronies—was unprepared to handle basic functions, let alone a massive relief and reconstruction effort. Relief that was supposed to be spent on food, medicine, housing, and schools was siphoned off at every level. Some estimated that only ten to twenty percent of the aid actually reached the poor.

This problem was not unique to Bangladesh. Globally, vast amounts of foreign aid, like wealth from natural resources, have ended up enriching elites in poor countries and subsidizing businesses in wealthy ones. A great deal of aid money has gone to pay high-priced Western consultants whose advice and decisions affect countless lives in developing countries. Although many consultants fly in and out of countries too quickly to gain a meaningful understanding of local cultures or conditions, they are rarely held accountable for wasteful or harmful programs that stem from their recommendations.

In Bangladesh, the influx of aid snowballed, until it came to represent 90 percent of the country's development budget. Billions of dollars were spent on projects—road construction, electricity generation, and agriculture development—that were prioritized by foreign donors and made sense on paper but often fell apart on the ground or produced benefits that bypassed the poor. The legacy of this aid is a culture of dependency and corruption that continues to distort Bangladesh's economy and government.

However, foreign aid did support some highly positive changes in Bangladesh when it was deployed to help finance— but not to control—citizen organizations that were founded by local social entrepreneurs. The two most famous examples are the Grameen Bank (the "Village Bank") and the Bangladesh Rural Advancement Committee (now known as BRAC).

After the war of independence, Bangladeshis around the world had abandoned lucrative careers in order to help rebuild their country. Among this group were Muhammad Yunus and Fazle H. Abed. Yunus, an economics professor who had completed a PhD at Vanderbilt University in the United States, established the Grameen Bank, a for-profit, antipoverty bank whose majority shareholders were the women villagers it served. Abed, a former executive at Shell Oil, founded BRAC, a nonprofit organization involved in rural education, health care, microfinance, and social and economic development.

At the time, aid was heavily paternalistic. The relationships between donors and recipients carried overtones from colonialism. By contrast, Grameen and BRAC operated under the presumption that Bangladeshis were capable, and they sought to build capacity and self-reliance within the country. They focused not just on material poverty but on dignity, eschewing charity in favor of respectful transactions.

Instead of hiring foreigners, they hired locals, and rather than dole out jobs to family friends, as was a commonplace practice, they hired staff members through competitive processes. And they refused to turn a blind eye to bribery, something many aid donors did in order to get their projects moving. Most of all, they were single-mindedly focused on efficiency and results. They counted and measured everything: every loan granted and repaid, every female child educated, every package of oral rehydration salts distributed. They tried to be responsive to their clients and prided themselves on their ability to help villagers recover quickly after natural disasters.

To develop solutions, they experimented continuously. Each launched countless variations on microfinance and rural enterprise development. BRAC led the way in Bangladesh, creating high-performing village-based schools and community health programs. In *Freedom from Want*, Ian Smillie examines how Abed opened up space in BRAC for staff members to take risks, pursue innovative ideas, and share their learning widely within the organization—while maintaining tight quality control. Both Yunus and Abed had the advantage of knowing they were in business for the long haul. They knew that if an idea or program failed, they could shut it down, absorb the lesson, and try something else. And many failures did ensue; some even grew into crises. But they used the failures as opportunities to think deeper about how to solve the country's problems. Foreign aid workers typically had little time for trial and error. Like politicians, they needed success in two-year cycles, because that was the average stint before they moved on.

Although aid donors had only sporadic exposure to Bangladesh, they often tried to impose their development ideas on Grameen and BRAC. Both organizations revolted, essentially saying: You can decide not to fund us. But you *cannot* touch our management. When it comes to Bangladesh, we know best.

Such defiance from recipients was unheard of. At the time, however, the aid industry was experiencing a backlash, and donors were feeling vulnerable. Journalists and other researchers had begun examining the track record of the so-called lords of poverty and revealing it to be unremarkable at best and disastrous at worst. To maintain political viability in their home countries, donors began hunting for organizations that could deliver results. Grameen and BRAC were the top contenders. They were meeting with striking success and had demonstrated the capacity to grow and maintain quality.

During the 1980s and 1990s, the Grameen Bank and BRAC used their bargaining leverage to negotiate unprecedented financing terms. They pressed donors, mostly governmental and multilateral aid agencies, to commit hundreds of millions of dollars in grants, low-cost loans, and loan guarantees to finance expansions. Never before had social entrepreneurs received funding on this scale. Moreover, the funding came as upfront capital, like investments, which allowed the organizations to execute against their own multiyear growth plans. The results were a world apart from anything the field of international development had yet seen.

Grameen and BRAC reached national scale in Bangladesh, each employing tens of thousands of staff members whose work touched the lives of tens of millions of Bangladeshis in almost every one of the nation's seventy thousand villages. Like great businesses, as they grew, they *improved*, adding new services, using technology more effectively, and spawning imitations. They built cultures of pride and optimism.

Today, despite Bangladesh's enduring poverty, its continuing saga of corruption and factional violence, and its vulnerability to cyclones and floods, the country has managed to expand its economy, reduce poverty by half, achieve significant improvements in maternal and child health, and increase rates of primary education. Except for Sri Lanka, it is the only South Asian country that has achieved parity in school access between girls and boys. Close to a fifth of Union Parishad officials (locally elected government administrators) come from families served by the Grameen Bank or BRAC. In recent national elections, more women voted than men.

The Grameen Bank and BRAC demonstrated that it was possible to mitigate poverty on a massive scale. They achieved new levels of success by departing from the historical pattern of social problem solving. Rather than implement preset policies through bureaucracies in a top-down fashion, they *grew* solutions from the bottom in a process characterized by trial and error, continuous iteration, and a sharp focus on results.

Together, these organizations helped shift the global development paradigm. They showed that the poor were powerful agents, not just needy beneficiaries. And they demonstrated the dramatic benefits of placing women, rather than male heads of households, at the center of development processes.

Over the past twenty years, thousands of development experts, academics, journalists, businesspeople, policy makers, and philanthropists have come to Bangladesh to apprentice themselves in a place that some call the Silicon Valley of social innovation. Yunus and Abed have traveled around the globe speaking to countless audiences and launched spinoff organizations to spread their work in dozens of countries. Microfinance, an idea that was treated as a crazy experiment twenty-five years ago, is now a global industry.

Although Grameen and BRAC behaved more like successful businesses than social programs, people didn't explicitly refer to Yunus and Abed as "social entrepreneurs" until the term was popularized by the organization Ashoka during the 1980s and 1990s. Ashoka, a global organization headquartered in Arlington, Virginia, was founded in 1980 by Bill Drayton, an American who had previously worked as a management consultant and an assistant administrator in the Environmental Protection Agency.

During the 1960s and 1970s, Drayton had traveled extensively in India, where he was influenced by the work of leaders such as Gandhi, Vinoba Bhave (founder of the "land gift" movement), and Verghese Kurien (architect of the "white revolution," which transformed dairy production). Each of these individuals had built organizations that realized radical visions for change.

What Drayton saw in his travels was that Indians across the country were doing the same. A generation after independence,

Indians were feeling more confident and assertive about their future. They were building organizations at every level to address social ills that had been ignored. Drayton spoke with many groups advocating ideas to reform Indian society— everything from improving sanitation to encouraging political participation from low-caste groups to creating new legal structures to protect the rights of women. Not all the groups were effective. He began to spot a pattern: the organizations that were making a difference had both a good idea and an unusually committed, creative, and action-oriented person at the helm: an idea champion or entrepreneur. He believed that these entrepreneurs had enormous potential to lead change efforts, but they were hobbled by many factors: they didn't have much money; they were misunderstood by their families and friends; and they often felt vulnerable and insignificant, isolated from one another and largely ignored by the media, the business sector, and the government.

He envisioned an organization that could support them. He named it after an Indian emperor, Ashoka, who lived roughly 2,200 years ago and is considered by many historians to be among the most benevolent and practical rulers in history. Some of Ashoka's ancient administrative reforms anticipated twentieth-century public works programs like those of the New Deal.

Drayton's organization began searching for social entrepreneurs in India in the early 1980s and, shortly thereafter, in Indonesia and Brazil. The goal was to lend financial support, credibility, and the strength of a global fellowship to entrepreneurs like Yunus and Abed at the moment when their work was poised to "take off." As a former management consultant, Drayton also recognized the need to build bridges between the social sector and the world of business, which historically had attracted most of society's entrepreneurs. Drayton and his colleagues developed a process for identifying "Fellows" using structured interviews that examined lifelong behavior patterns, the social impact of their ideas, the creativity of their problem solving, and their trustworthiness and personal integrity. Over the past three decades, Ashoka has supported more than two thousand Fellows from seventy countries, many of whom have achieved social impact at national and international levels.

Since the 1980s, many other organizations have emerged which have played critical roles building the field of social entrepreneurship. The New York–based Echoing Green Foundation has supported nearly five hundred early-stage social entrepreneurs from forty countries, inspiring many to pursue this career out of college. New Profit, Inc., based in Boston, was one of the first groups to meet the need for growth funding among high-impact organizations in the United States. In recent years, it has also led the way in strengthening the relationship between social entrepreneurs and U.S. policy makers. The Geneva-based Schwab Foundation for Social Entrepreneurship has raised the profile of social entrepreneurs in the international business community and media through its linkages to the World Economic Forum and its awards programs. And the Skoll Foundation has played a central role drawing international attention to the work of social entrepreneurs through its media efforts, its global award and fellowship programs, and its annual Skoll World Forum held at Oxford University, which has become the flagship event in the field.

What does a social entrepreneur do?

We are surrounded by good ideas and effective models: we know how to teach disadvantaged kids to read, reduce energy consumption, and improve health care while reducing its cost. We even know how to eliminate much of the bullying that takes place in school yards. At some level, all of these problems are being solved in the United States and Canada today. But what we don't know how to do is to take the knowledge we possess in bits and pieces and implement it at the scale of the problems we are facing. Many, if not most, international development and government schemes begin with impressive pilot projects and end with disappointing results. In their article "Social Entrepreneurship: The Case for Definition," Roger L. Martin and Sally Osberg argue that the role of the social entrepreneur is to move society from a "stable but inherently unjust equilibrium" to a "new, stable equilibrium" that releases potential and alleviates suffering on a major scale. Social entrepreneurs work to ensure that sensible ideas take root and actually change people's thinking and behavior across a society.

Reforms at this level frequently require systems to change, which has always been extraordinarily difficult. Six hundred years ago, in *The Prince*, Niccolò Machiavelli observed:

> [T]here is nothing more difficult to take in hand, more perilous to conduct, or more uncertain in its success, than to take the lead in the introduction of a new order of things. Because the innovator has for enemies all those who have done well under the old conditions, and lukewarm defenders in those who may do well under the new. This coolness arises partly from fear of the opponents, who have the laws on their side, and partly from the incredulity of men, who do not readily believe in new things until they have had a long experience of them.

The system changer must therefore overcome apathy, habit, incomprehension, and disbelief while facing heated resistance from those with vested interests. Social entrepreneurs have to figure out how to make it happen.

Given the difficulties, it's easy to understand why serious problems *don't* get solved more readily in modern democracies, where governments balance the conflicting interests of millions of people, including powerful elites, while under intense scrutiny to produce short-term results.

Consider the absurd demands we make on our governments. Policy makers must appear decisive and resolute, with ready answers at their fingertips for all manner of problems. An open and deliberative problem-solving approach, informed by trial and error, is practically impossible to institutionalize in such an environment. As a result, policies tend to be shaped by executive or legislative staff members who are removed from the details of implementation yet under intense time pressures to come up with comprehensive solutions or "plans." Consequentially, national policies are regularly based on assumptions that get tested largely after they become law.

Anyone who has tried to advance a change that runs counter to the interests of well-organized groups—the oil or bank lobbies, the teachers union, or the National Rifle Association, for example—knows how routinely promising ideas are killed without fair hearings. Americans are worried that their banking, health, education, and criminal justice systems are profoundly inadequate for today's challenges. Few disagree about the need for reform, yet many insiders battle to defend the status quo.

New ideas are often rejected by the very people who stand to benefit from them, especially if they feel imposed upon or baffled by the proposed changes. One of the biggest problems in the field of information technology is "system rejection": employees simply refuse to use new computer systems that companies have spent billions to develop. In public education, about half of all new teachers leave the profession within five years, which is another form of system rejection. Yet their unions, protective of hard-won battles, frequently stand in the way of reforms that might bring successful educators more job satisfaction and better pay.

Many ideas get off to a good start but get watered down in the implementation. The problem may be that the agency or institution advancing the idea is unable to grow and maintain quality, one of the toughest organizational challenges. Perhaps it can't afford to hire people who have experience managing growth. When quality deteriorates, motivation wanes. Or perhaps a crisis strikes—a political upheaval, a stock market plunge, a natural disaster—and a fragile organization is washed away before it is able to establish roots.

There are countless unforeseeable dangers that can kill a good idea. From the perspective of a theoretician, a new idea may be interesting in and of itself. From the perspective of an entrepreneur, it makes no sense to talk about an idea without talking about the details of implementation, which include such things as how to finance the work, how to motivate staff and clients, and perhaps how to build a political constituency or engage organized opponents. And the answers, of course, are always changing.

If an important new idea is to achieve major social impact, it needs a force to drive it forward that can be counted upon to provide the care, energy, resourcefulness, and stubbornness necessary to navigate the idea through the system. Social entrepreneurs must attract attention and funding, overcome apathy and opposition, shift behavior and mobilize political will, continually improve the idea, and take care of all the details in painstaking fashion, no matter how long it takes.

Ashoka's key insight was that if you want to predict how things will turn out for a new idea, your best bet is to focus on the person behind the idea. Does the person have the ability and motivation to guide a team that can overcome what may be an inexhaustible supply of obstacles, setbacks and heartbreaks? Is the realization of the idea the most important thing in the world for this person, or close?

In the cases of the Grameen Bank and BRAC, Yunus and Abed had each embarked on long struggles marked by disappointments and setbacks. In the beginning, they were very much alone. People told Yunus that the Grameen Bank would burst "like a balloon." Others told Abed that he was foolish to leave his high-paying job at Shell Oil. Both experienced personal losses. Both had to contend with religious fundamentalists, military dictators, socialist revolutionaries, and, perhaps toughest of all, a habit of corruption that sapped the trust out of every transaction. Both worked intentionally to "market" their ideas, repeating the same stories over and over to help mobilize resources, form partnerships, disarm enemies, and woo political power brokers. Both were committed to seeing this process through to its end, even if it took their whole lives.

The role of the social entrepreneur can be understood through these examples. Social entrepreneurs initiate and lead change processes that are self-correcting, growth-oriented, and impact-focused. They create new configurations of people and coordinate their efforts to attack problems more successfully than before. It's a complex role that involves a great deal of listening, recruiting, and persuading. It takes a curious combination of sensitivity and bullheadedness, humility and audacity, and restlessness and patience to lead a change process in the face of indifference, habit, fear, resource constraints, vested interest, and institutional defenses.

The job can be boiled down to one essential function: the social entrepreneur helps others to envision a new possibility, appreciate its meaning, and recognize how it can be broken down into doable steps that build momentum for change.

The process described above can't work if people lack a sense of ownership for the change. It can't work if there is insufficient space for experimentation or if people are unwilling to talk about failure. It can't work if the daily pressures make it impossible to stay focused on the long-term goal. If we consider the structural constraints in different sectors, the need for social entrepreneurship becomes abundantly clear. A business that doesn't promise profits within five to seven years will not attract conventional investment, no matter how important its products. An idea that doesn't fit within the political shutter speed will face an uphill battle in government. (It's easier to get politicians to spend money on incarceration than on early childhood education.) To orchestrate positive long-term changes, we need people who think beyond quarterly reports and news and election cycles, and who persist in the absence of short-term rewards or recognition. We need people who possess a ground-level view of problems and a mountaintop vision, who have a talent for building teams and the freedom to experiment. We need natural institution builders who care more about solving social problems than becoming personally wealthy.

Finally, it's important to reemphasize that social entrepreneurship is a *process* that involves more than the founders of organizations. Many extraordinary people work closely with social entrepreneurs for years without receiving public recognition, including many "intrapreneurs," who drive considerable innovation within their organizations. Examples include Dipal Chandra Barua in the Grameen Bank, Aminul

Alam in BRAC, and Sushmita Ghosh in Ashoka. To be sure, founders play central roles initiating and navigating changes processes and marketing ideas. They receive the lion's share of awards and media attention, but they accomplish little by themselves.

What are social entrepreneurs like?

Social entrepreneurs come from all walks of life. Some begin their careers as doctors, engineers, teachers, priests, social workers, clowns, journalists, computer programmers, artists, nurses, businesspeople, and architects. Some get pulled into their work because of friendship or family crises. The Ashoka Fellowship offers the most comprehensive view of the global field of social entrepreneurship. At a gathering of Ashoka Fellows, you might find a twenty-four-year-old factory worker from an Asian slum discussing growth strategies with a sixty-year-old Mexican banker in pinstripes. Next to them an Indian journalist in a wheelchair might be overheard exchanging organizing tactics with a Polish organic farmer, while listening in are an American defense attorney, a former professional surfer from Brazil, a South African pediatrician, and a Bangladeshi garment manufacturer. In the crowd would be MBAs from top universities and villagers with secondary school educations, people who work in laboratories, and people who spend their days where there is no electricity and no running water.

All of them share some basic temperamental qualities. For example, entrepreneurs are comfortable with uncertainty, have a high need for autonomy, and are biased toward action. However, entrepreneurs are not necessarily highly charismatic or confident. Research indicates that their success is less a function of inborn personality traits than the patterns of behavior they adopt. Although some people are born with more entrepreneurial inclination than others, the management expert Peter Drucker has argued that most people can learn to behave like entrepreneurs.

In particular, certain types of experiences seem to help people, especially children, discover their agency. Many social entrepreneurs can recall a time in childhood when they were actively encouraged by an adult to take initiative—to start a club or organize a league, for example—and then assisted in the process. The achievement taught them to value and act on their own ideas. Many also recall instances when they spoke up against injustice—called out a bully on the playground, for example, or pointed out a racial stereotype inadvertently used by a teacher—and discovered that they could make a difference. Those experiences were highly reinforcing.

Psychologists note that entrepreneurs score high on the quality "inner locus of control." They locate power within, rather than outside, themselves. If they don't have the skills to solve a problem, they believe they can acquire them by experimenting, by observing experts, or by getting help from others. When things go wrong, they want to know primarily what happened—and what needs to be fixed, not whom to blame. They don't take failure as an indication of personal inadequacy but as an indication of a gap in their understanding, something that can be remedied with more effort.

Social entrepreneurs frequently speak of an adult they were close to in childhood, usually a parent or other relative, who was highly ethical and had a profound influence on their thinking. They often refer to these relatives when explaining their inability to bypass the suffering of others. Many have vivid recollections of times when this adult guided or challenged them to understand injustice or question conventional beliefs. For example, Alice Tepper Marlin, the founder of Social Accountability International and one of the pioneers in the field of socially responsible business, grew up in a comfortable community in New Jersey. When she was in grade school, her father periodically took her to see New York City's Lower East Side, where poverty was highly concentrated and many people lived on the streets. Those experiences and conversations, which she found deeply moving, changed her understanding of the world.

The most common misconception about entrepreneurs is that they like to take risks. While researching his landmark book *The Achieving Society*, David McClelland found that entrepreneurs are attracted to challenges when the key determinant of success is skill, not chance. Entrepreneurs aren't gamblers, he wrote. In fact, they will go to extreme lengths to minimize or eliminate risks, painstakingly seeking information to increase the odds of success. They usually overestimate their chances of success, however, which is why others perceive them as risk takers.

Entrepreneurs tend to be good listeners. They must be able to identify with others so they can understand their motivations and bring them together into effective teams. Andrew Carnegie said that entrepreneurs must be willing to endure the "humbling eclipse of self" that comes from "profound learning from others." They tend to be open-minded and on the lookout for useful information. Goethe could have been describing entrepreneurs when he noted that "the person of analytic or critical intellect finds something ridiculous in everything" while "the person of synthetic or constructive intellect" finds something ridiculous "in almost nothing."

For people who are often exposed to extreme suffering, social entrepreneurs are surprisingly nonideological. Ideology can impede problem solving if it puts a filter on reality and causes a person to dismiss evidence that challenges his or her beliefs. Entrepreneurs intentionally cultivate relationships with people across political camps and from a variety of backgrounds so they can better understand how to navigate change. They will attend the World Economic Forum one year (if they can get in) and the World Social Forum the next.

To succeed, social entrepreneurs have to remain steadfast in the face of choruses of doubters and critics. This quality can have some downsides; it allows such people to ignore detractors but may cause them to disregard their own shortcomings or even their own desires. Some social entrepreneurs devote themselves so fully to their ideas that they never get around to marrying or having children, even though they once hoped to have families. And, having immersed themselves completely in their work, they sometimes have difficulty working closely with people who want to lead more balanced lives.

Many social entrepreneurs believe that they are fulfilling their life's purpose. For some, this conviction stems from a conscious faith. For others, it grows intuitively and slowly as they pursue different kinds of work until alighting on a vocation that expresses their values and talents. Some who have suffered a great loss or trauma derive meaning and comfort by working to relieve the pain of others or to prevent others from having to endure similar pain. Candice Lightner founded the group Mothers Against Drunk Driving after her thirteen-year-old daughter, Cari, was killed by a drunk driver who was a repeat offender. Leaders in the disability movement are frequently disabled themselves or have disabled children. Many doctors who have become social entrepreneurs did so after witnessing suffering that was not being alleviated through conventional medical models. A common pattern is for a person to take action to help a friend, relative or patient, only to discover others in similar circumstances. The person finds himself drawn deeper into the work and is unable to return to a previous way of living. For example, in their book *Be Bold*, Cheryl L. Dorsey and Lara Galinsky tell stories of twelve social entrepreneurs supported by Echoing Green who all experienced a "moment of obligation" that caused them to change course and pursue work of deep personal significance.

Finally, one quality not to be overlooked is the capacity to derive joy and celebrate small successes, even while the path ahead remains difficult. Social entrepreneurship is a long-term commitment, with many setbacks and disappointments. Those who stick it out and manage to recruit others always find ways to enjoy the journey.

What is the difference between social and business entrepreneurship?

The main difference has to do with purpose, or what the enterprise is trying to maximize. For social entrepreneurs, the bottom line is to maximize some form of social impact, usually by addressing an urgent need that is being mishandled, overlooked, or ignored by other institutions. For business entrepreneurs, the bottom line may be to maximize profits or shareholder wealth, or to build an ongoing, respected entity that provides value to customers and meaningful work to employees. The world needs both kinds of entrepreneurship; one should not be deemed superior to the other, although social entrepreneurship is often more challenging because it tackles problems that have defied governmental approaches and for which market solutions have not yet been demonstrated. And, of course, there are overlaps: social entrepreneurs often earn profits through social enterprises, and businesspeople are frequently concerned with social responsibility. Both types of entrepreneurship require vision, initiative, organization building and "marketing." In terms of skill and temperament, social and business entrepreneurs are strikingly similar. But their *primary* objectives are different.

People build enterprises to accomplish many different things. Some seek to build the world's dominant running shoe company, construct the world's fastest computers, or expand the market for subprime loans. Others want to create integrated housing for disabled people, develop vaccines for developing world diseases, or help poor children gain access to quality books. Some researchers argue that there is little use in making distinctions and that all entrepreneurs should be considered social entrepreneurs because they generate employment and meet needs. We disagree. We wouldn't call someone a social entrepreneur who introduced snacks like potato chips or Twinkies to the Chinese market, even if his or her firm generated a million jobs.

Seeking to maximize social impact is not the only criterion for social entrepreneurship. As Greg Dees noted, entrepreneurship involves elements of newness and dynamism. Today, thousands of "cleantech" and "greentech" companies are addressing environmental problems, but not all are examples of social entrepreneurship. Within the solar energy industry, for example, many firms sell established products in established markets. Without minimizing their contributions to the solution, it's useful to distinguish conventional firms from those that are pioneering new products, attempting to change industries, or building markets in particularly difficult contexts. The small firm D.light Design is a good example. In a world in which two billion people lack access to electricity, it is trying to market low-cost solar-electric lamps to villagers and slum dwellers in the developing world so they can switch from kerosene, an unhealthy and dangerous substance that contributes to global warming.

One of the leading examples of social entrepreneurship in the United States is ShoreBank Corporation, the nation's first community development and environmentally conscious bank holding company. Headquartered on Chicago's South Side, today ShoreBank is a $2.4 billion company with for-profit banks and social-purpose affiliates in five states, as well as global consulting and financing arms. It began by lending money to local businesspeople on the South Side of Chicago who rehabilitated the neighborhood's housing stock. If ShoreBank had set up shop in a middle-class community, we would simply call it a bank—a good bank, to be sure. But its founders intentionally opened in a poor area of Chicago that was reeling from the flight of the middle class, where banking services had become all but nonexistent. ShoreBank developed a business model attuned to the needs of this under-banked community and, in the process, helped transform it. The bank sought to maximize the social impact of its lending, while maintaining a healthy profit margin. Had ShoreBank sought to maximize profits, it would have done what many other banks did at the time: abandon the inner cities. Instead, it became the *only* bank to support the landmark Community Reinvestment Act, which aimed to halt the redlining of poor neighborhoods.

Moreover, two of ShoreBank's founders, Ron Grzywinski and Mary Houghton, took several trips to Bangladesh to share their banking experiences with officials of the Grameen Bank and BRAC. Through ShoreBank's affiliated nonprofit arm, Yunus and a senior BRAC manager traveled to the United

States in exchanges that led to the establishment of microfinance programs in several U.S. states and attracted the attention of key policy makers, notably Bill and Hillary Clinton, then governor and first lady of Arkansas, who carried their support for microfinance into the White House.

Social entrepreneurship has to be understood also in relation to the evolution of thinking and practice in a given field. What is innovative in one generation may be conventional or even retrograde in the next. Microfinance began as an example of social entrepreneurship, but now these services are being extended by formal financial institutions primarily interested in profitability. Commercial banks have entered this market following thirty years of work by path breakers who demonstrated its viability. The people who broke ground didn't get wealthy; some depleted personal savings to build their organizations. Now commercial microfinance promises to open up huge capital flows for financing small loans. The banks' efforts, if handled responsibly, could benefit hundreds of millions of people, perhaps billions. In our view, however, banks practice social entrepreneurship only when they seek to maximize social impact rather than profitability. The test is what they do when faced to choose between the two objectives. Do they overlook poorer borrowers in favor of wealthier ones? Do they charge the poor interest rates that are substantially higher than their own cost of capital? The current mortgage crisis occurred because banks were so concerned with profits they neglected the social consequences of their lending. A similar crisis in microfinance could produce suffering around the globe.

For generations, business entrepreneurs have outnumbered and received more attention than social entrepreneurs. The top business entrepreneurs benefited from robust financial and managerial services, which allowed them to build phenom-enally successful companies. They generated tremendous excitement; many became legends. By contrast, the social entrepreneurs contended with unpredictable and fragmented financing. Their organizations grew slowly. The founders did not appear on *Forbes* lists. Media companies did not create magazines devoted to their activities. They didn't even get their own newspaper beats. Next to business and government leaders, their role went unnoticed.

But that is changing. Today the attention meter is angling in the direction of social entrepreneurship as more people are asking themselves the question at its heart: What kind of enterprise is *worth* devoting your life to build?

What are the differences between social entrepreneurship and government?

We often reduce social entrepreneurship to stories of char-ismatic people. As we have mentioned, social entrepreneur-ship describes a *process*, a way to organize problem-solving efforts. The entrepreneurial authors get the ball rolling, but the process has its own characteristics.

Unlike governmental efforts, it flows from the bottom up. Typically it grows out of one person's direct interaction with a problem and a simple question: "Hey, what if we tried X?" What follows is an experiment, a response, some adjust-ment, and more experimentation. Over time, the entrepreneur accumulates experience. He or she works to attract resources and usually has to persuade people to abandon conventional careers in order to join a small team of people committed to an unproven idea. At the outset, the process requires unusual levels of commitment. It also requires humility and faith, because in most cases, early efforts are small, fraught with error, and take years to show significant results. If the process is successful, what emerges is a new institution whose staff, board members, and supporters bring together the skills, knowledge, and influence to advance a new approach.

Social entrepreneurs don't control major resources, and, unlike governments, they can't command compliance. They have to leverage resources that others control and influence people by articulating goals that are meaningful. Social entrepreneurs are most effective when they demonstrate ideas that inspire others to go out and create their own social change. The beauty of demonstrating positive pathways is that it is possible to redirect human energy without telling people what to do. Consider the spread of microfinance, charter schools, and independent living centers, which have been taken up by people working independently around the world. People have embraced these ideas because they offer opportunities to be effective.

Social entrepreneurship is inductive and outward-looking: it moves from observation and experimentation to institutionalization and independent adoption. As a rule, major initiatives advanced by governments and international aid agencies flow in the reverse direction, beginning with policy battles and ending with programs planned and implemented through agencies or contracted to service providers. This approach has its own characteristics. Public policies often lack a nuanced appreciation for ground-level details. Rules and procedures designed to prevent corruption or waste, or to ensure fairness, often limit flexibility and responsiveness. Another characteristic is that any modification at the local level may involve a long approval process.

Even when policies are flawed, it takes a monumental effort to correct them. Once a program is rolled out, with a budget and a constituency to defend that budget, it will remain there almost regardless of its effectiveness. The primary feedback mechanisms for policy makers—press reports and elections— punish failure and demand results in unrealistically short time frames. Consequentially, elected officials come to favor the short-term appearance of success over actual success. This dynamic understandably distorts policy making.

Social entrepreneurs are less encumbered by these constraints, which accounts for their competitive advantage in devising solutions. They can try out crazy ideas and hire and fire people based solely on performance. They can recruit talented executives more easily than government (assuming they can pay them) because nobody has to worry about being attacked in the press for joining a citizen organization. (Many executives cringe at the thought of putting themselves forward for high-level government posts.) Most of all, social entrepreneurs have the luxury to work on problems until they figure them out, provided they can find someone to foot the bill. Often, groundbreaking strategic insights don't come for years, as was the case with the Grameen Bank, which began making loans primarily to women after seven years of experimentation lending mainly to men.

These structural differences explain why social entrepreneurs are so inventive and highly motivated and why committed people in government often feel frustrated and hamstrung.

Governments can be innovative, of course, especially when institutional entrepreneurs, or intrapreneurs, are given leeway to innovate. The possibilities for changing public structures from within have been demonstrated by such people as Francis Perkins, the architect of much of the New Deal; Sargent Shriver, who launched the Peace Corps; John Gardner, who led President Johnson's Department of Health, Education and Welfare and later established the White House Fellows Program and the public interest lobby Common Cause; and James Grant, the former head of UNICEF who led massive efforts to disseminate vaccines and oral rehydration therapy, preventing the deaths of tens of million of children.

Like business entrepreneurship, social entrepreneurship carries risks. Just as nobody can predict where the next eBay, Google, or Twitter will come from, nobody can predict where the best solutions to tough social problems will emerge. To produce a steady steam of social innovations, we need to actively search for social entrepreneurs with the same seriousness and vigor that investors like Warren Buffett devote to finding and building undervalued companies. This approach, which can be undertaken equally by governments and other social investors, will naturally produce many social ventures that fail, some that perform well, and a few that cause transformative change. Society needs to encourage and harness decentralized social experimentation on a larger scale and far more systematically than it currently does. Governments, in particular, would benefit by focusing more on spotting and supporting talented changemakers outside their walls.

To address problems at the necessary scale, we need to interweave the creativity, agility, and operational excellence found in the field of social entrepreneurship with the resources and legitimacy of governments.

How is social entrepreneurship different from activism?

Activism can be thought of as a subset of social entrepreneurship, one of many tactics employed to advance change. The simplest distinction is that activists generally seek to elicit change by influencing the decision making of large institutions or by changing public attitudes, while social entrepreneurs pursue a wider range of options, including building institutions that directly implement solutions themselves.

Many social entrepreneurs incorporate activism in their work, crafting campaigns to induce change in governments, corporations, universities, or bodies like the World Trade Organization. Groups such as 1Sky, 350.org, and the Energy Action Coalition are organizing hundreds of thousands of people to change U.S. environmental policies in response to global warming. The Genocide Intervention Network has organized thousands of student activists who pressure governments to respond more forcefully to mass atrocities in Darfur, the Democratic Republic of Congo, and other countries. In recent decades, activists have been primary actors in movements seeking to ban landmines and to advance legal protections for women, gays, racial minorities, and people with disabilities.

Activism and direct problem solving go hand in hand. In the field of disability, for example, early social entrepreneurs built schools for people with visual and hearing impairments and adapted learning environments for people with other disabilities. In recent decades, they created accessible workplaces and independent living centers. These innovations broke new ground and demonstrated that disabled people could live more independent and satisfying lives—and could be far better integrated with mainstream society—than had previously been imagined. But most were relatively small, privately funded organizations, and they were far from a comprehensive solution to disability discrimination. Advocates saw that as long as public schools, universities, and businesses were permitted by law to systematically exclude students and employees purely on the basis of a disability, the disabled would remain marginal.

In the 1970s, therefore, disability groups established new organizations that explicitly focused on activism rather than service delivery, with the dual goals of spreading awareness about the conditions of people with disabilities and changing laws and standards across society. One early group, Disability in Action, attracted national attention by occupying a floor in a federal office building for 25 days in 1977. The attention led the U.S. government to pass the nation's first regulations banning discrimination against the disabled in any federally funded institution or government contractor. In 1990, many of the same activists won passage of the landmark Americans with Disabilities Act.

Activists bring political or consumer pressure to bear by showing their numbers and their intensity, and thereby forcing elected officials, business executives, or other leaders to heed their demands and attend to their grievances. As a long-term change strategy, however, the greatest power of activism may not be its ability to compel action but its capacity to elicit empathy by making injustice and suffering palpable. There is no better example of this than Gandhi's 1930 Salt March, which dramatized the injustice of colonial rule by focusing on what appeared to be a tiny prohibition: the law that forbade Indians from making their own salt.

It was a seemingly simple plan: Gandhi announced his intention to make salt and spent days walking from his inland ashram to the Bombay salt flats on the Indian Ocean. He knew his 241-mile walk would slowly build suspense and that it would culminate in a confrontation with the colonial authority. When he finally arrived at the sea, before tens of thousands of witnesses, including many journalists, Gandhi bent down, picked up some salt, held it aloft, and was promptly arrested.

More than sixty thousand Indians repeated his act. Many were subsequently beaten bloody by soldiers working for the British authorities. The activists refused to fight back and the images of dignified men and women being brutally clubbed by soldiers circulated around the globe. The effect was to bring into sharp focus the moral deformity of colonialism.

Years later, American civil rights activists, led by Martin Luther King Jr., followed Gandhi's lead as they marched peacefully in the streets of the South, singing and holding hands, while phalanxes of police, armed with riot gear and clubs, vicious dogs and fire hoses, set upon them in brutal attacks. Scholars have argued that the images of these confrontations, beamed into millions of homes, were critical in opening the hearts of millions to the plight of American blacks.

One fundamental difference between today's social entrepreneurs and yesterday's activists is that, historically, activists have proceeded largely as outsiders to power—like uninvited guests storming the gates of the mansion. By contrast, social entrepreneurs frequently combine outside- and inside-oriented tactics to bring change. In recent years, for example, social entrepreneurs in the environmental movement have engaged directly with companies such as Wal-Mart and General Electric, as well as the U.S. Army, to teach environmentally positive practices. Outside activists have convinced companies that they need to change, while social entrepreneurs working on the inside have shown them what to do.

This points to a central insight of social entrepreneurship: institutions on the receiving end of pressure are frequently at a loss about how to respond to demands for change. For example, environmental activists often assume that corporate executives know how to modify their business practices and remain profitable. But in the face of new environmental and global economic pressures, many business leaders are bewildered and defensive. To get them to break with the past, it's not enough to condemn them or boycott their companies. We must show them how to build the future. We must advise or compete with them.

This dimension—the constructive element of change—is too often overlooked by would be changemakers. Consider the field of education. To be sure, political mobilization is essential to reform education policies. But today we need to figure out how to build systems to identify, retain, and nurture effective teachers and ensure that ineffective teachers are rerouted to other careers as quickly as possible. For this, we need demonstrated solutions, not just political power. Accordingly, a kind of activism is emerging that is more concerned with problem solving than voicing outrage. As *New York Times* columnist Nicholas D. Kristof has observed: "I'm struck that while there has always been student activism, it was mostly protest in my day, while these days it often includes an element of starting an organization to do something positive as well. It's the social entrepreneurship revolution, and I'm in awe of it."

What is the relationship between social entrepreneurship and democracy?

Democracies flourish when large numbers of citizens acquire the capacity to shape civic life. Social entrepreneurship is a process by which citizens organize to do just that. To the degree that a significant percentage of people—not just a few appointed or elected elites—are engaged in leadership efforts to address problems, and to the degree that they know how to be effective, they will feel more confident and powerful as citizens, and the society will be more adaptive and resilient.

The history of the United States is full of examples of social entrepreneurs who have strengthened democracy. People like William Lloyd Garrison, Susan B. Anthony, Booker T. Washington, and the disability advocate Judith E. Heumann collaborated in building institutions that made it possible for Americans to acquire and express their power as citizens and thus shape their own history. Similarly, half a decade after the Berlin Wall fell, Ashoka found social entrepreneurs emerging in large numbers across Eastern Europe. They had already started building new schools and environmental organizations to replace the bureaucracies that had dominated under Communism.

Democracy is a process of continual adaptation, as citizens experiment in the building of institutions to meet their needs at different moments in history. During the twentieth century, for example, citizens in wealthy democracies pressed their governments to construct an array of new public goods and safety nets, such as publicly funded education, social security, and health care for the poor and elderly. They greatly expanded the role of the government, which became a provider and third-party purchaser of many services.

But in recent decades, it has become clear that that many of those services have fallen short of their goals: for example, many public schools fail to educate significant numbers of students, most foster care systems do not prepare youth for successful adulthood, and the criminal justice system routinely turns minor offenders into career criminals. Citizens have responded by building a new array of institutions to try to fix the problems that emerged out of the solutions developed by previous generations. Abraham Lincoln saw the evolution of the nation as an iterative process, with each new generation standing on the shoulders of the previous one, striving to bring society a little closer to its founding ideals of freedom and equality.

Today, for example, we see groups like the Memphis-based Youth Villages improving the foster care model through family-based treatments. Foster care was itself an improvement over the earlier state of affairs, in which youths from troubled families were often sent to work houses as indentured servants. That in turn was believed to have been an improvement over the practice of placing children in almshouses, which had a history of neglect and abuse.

Over the past thirty years, social entrepreneurs operating globally have also demonstrated that in predemocratic contexts or in the context of fragile democracies, their work builds skills and attitudes that can ignite and reinforce citizen power. Each time a citizen stands up and acts effectively to address a problem, others are emboldened. People first come to believe that change is possible, and then they learn how to advance change themselves.

That happened in Brazil in the early 1980s. While the country was still under military rule, social entrepreneurs began encouraging citizens to challenge government and business hegemony. Chico Mendes and Mary Allegretti organized indigenous people and rubber tappers to protest the burning and cutting of the Amazon rain forest, leading others to demand protections in the Pantanal and later the Atlantic Rainforest. In Bahia, the cultural group Olodum demonstrated that Carnival could be used as a force for the educational, economic, and political advancement of Afro-Brazilians, inspiring many black communities across Brazil to transform local cultural organizations into vehicles for economic and political change.

Similarly, in the 1970s and 1980s in Eastern Europe, environmentalists seeking to protect primeval forests, natural river systems, and endangered species laid much of the organizational groundwork for the citizen action that culminated in the fall of the Berlin Wall in 1989. (Today, the environmental movement remains at the forefront of citizen activity in China.) The numerous citizen organizations in Brazil and Eastern Europe solidify past gains and make it difficult for dictatorships to reemerge.

In wealthy democracies, social entrepreneurs spend as much time renewing old institutions as they do building new ones. In poor, weak, or failed states, however, social entrepreneurs are more often focused on basic needs which people in Western democracies take for granted. In India, for example, despite remarkable economic growth, more than 40 percent of the children are underweight. Many social entrepreneurs there and in other developing countries focus on expanding access to safe drinking water, providing primary health care and education, delivering electricity, and promoting improved sanitation and nutrition. These are considered public goods in developed countries.

One significant demographic difference is that the poor are in the majority in developing countries, so poverty is a central political issue. Thus, social entrepreneurs can gain access to policy makers more easily. The big constraint they face is resources. In developed countries, the poor are in the minority, and their concerns are frequently ignored by policy makers. The constraint there is not money but political will. To get the attention of policy makers, social entrepreneurs have to learn how to compete head to head with well-financed lobbyists and any number of special interest groups.

In the poorest parts of the world, which tend also to be the least democratic, social entrepreneurs have difficulty operating at any level of scale. In *The Bottom Billion*, Paul Collier notes that the poorest billion people in the world usually live in countries characterized by violent conflict, overdependence on natural resources, physical isolation, and catastrophic governance. In such contexts, state services are frequently corrupt, ineffective, or nonexistent, and violence is commonplace. Citizen organizations may provide basic education, health care, or economic development, but rarely on anything more than a modest scale. It is difficult for social entrepreneurship to flourish without a baseline of security and social order. BRAC is now the largest provider of microfinance and other services in Afghanistan, but its gains have come at great cost. Several of its staff members have been kidnapped and murdered.

As the field of social entrepreneurship continues to expand, it may foreshadow a new stage of democracy—one animated by citizens who are actively involved in building, shaping, and renewing organizations to improve society. As such, it may also come to redefine citizenship.

In the United States and Canada, we practice what could be called a minimalist type of citizenship. A good citizen votes, pays taxes, abides by the law, and serves in the military when called. Anything beyond that—volunteering, say, or being helpful to neighbors or addressing social problems—is considered optional (though it is esteemed). Even our core duties are fairly passive: voting is essentially a process of giving away power, only a relative few serve in the military, and most of us pay taxes grudgingly.

What we don't have is a collective belief that with citizenship comes a responsibility to serve society. Some advocates of national service hope to see Congress one day pass a law requiring every citizen or resident to engage in public service for a year or two. Currently, the political constituency does not exist in the United States and Canada to move this idea forward. Beyond taxation to pay for the social safety net, we don't ask or expect citizens to assume responsibility for the well-being of anyone outside their families.

It's worth asking how modern democracies have evolved to accept individualistic social norms that would cause tribal societies, military units, and sports teams to collapse. Part of the answer may stem from Adam Smith's famous notion of the "hidden hand" and how it may have influenced our understanding of the relationship between the individual and society.

The hidden hand describes the mysterious process by which markets coordinate economic behavior. Smith argued that large numbers of individuals, each pursuing their own narrow profit seeking, will unintentionally maximize the wealth of all. In many cases, he was right. The hidden hand metaphor has a significant drawback, however. It transforms self-interest into a public virtue, releasing citizens from the need to consider the whole of society and effectively shrinking everyone's circle of accountability. This idea, perhaps the most influential in the history of economics, may be the basis for the questionable modern notion that individuals need only assume responsibility for themselves in order to enjoy social well-being.

Citizenship could be construed differently. We might define a good citizen as one who takes an active and intentional role in the shaping of a good society, both at an individual and communal level. The Founding Fathers didn't just look after their own economic interests; they built institutions to realize their vision for a new nation. In so doing, they demonstrated the power and responsibilities of citizenship. Today, the example they set can be seen in contemporary form in the field of social entrepreneurship, with hands-on institution building and problem solving emerging as a more common expression of citizenship.

These changes are driven by the failure of old institutions to meet the needs of our time. In a world of lightning change, more people need to be involved in solving problems. A thriving economy requires that many people build new businesses and serve them in different ways; an adaptive society requires that many people construct and collaborate on solutions. Today, we can see that a hidden hand coordinates more than just profit seeking; it also coordinates solution seeking as change agents respond to new problems and new opportunities. For example, the market signals of urgent needs and lowered "barriers to entry" have fueled a global explosion of environmental organizations and, domestically, a surge of social entrepreneurship in education and health care.

A vision of robust citizenship is captured beautifully by John Gardner, in his book *Self-Renewal*: "[S]ociety is not like a machine that is created at some point in time and then maintained with a minimum of effort; it is being continuously re-created, for good or ill, by its members. This will strike some as a burdensome responsibility, but it will summon others to greatness."

II

CHALLENGES OF CAUSING CHANGE

What are the main financial constraints?

It is often assumed that start-up capital is a significant hurdle for social entrepreneurs. Although it is never easy to obtain the initial investment or grant funding for a new idea, most social entrepreneurs have less trouble in getting started than taking off. The major constraint is the difficulty in accessing growth capital.

Unlike business entrepreneurs, who, once proven, can raise money from well-established capital markets through debt or stock issues, social entrepreneurs running nonprofit organizations are financed by foundations, philanthropists, or governments whose typical investments are modest in size and relatively short-term (the average grant term is one year). Some revenue-generating social enterprises have accessed capital from impact investors (who seek financial goals and social impact). But markets for this kind of financing are still in their embryonic stages. Only a handful of foundations provide large pools of growth capital for social organizations, while governments, which have sufficient resources to finance significant expansion, prefer to pay for services as they are delivered, rather than invest in building institutions.

Social entrepreneurs running small or medium-size organizations pursue government funding with reluctance because of the difficulty in complying with government reporting requirements. To qualify for funding, groups also may have to reshape themselves to fit standardized guidelines. And the funding is unpredictable, often contingent more on politics than performance.

For these reasons, many social entrepreneurs prefer to raise money from philanthropists. Here they run into a different set of problems. Philanthropists can be more flexible, but each has unique application procedures and reporting formats. With little standardization, fund-raising is time-consuming and expensive. And, again, funding is not always linked to results. Mediocre organizations with strong brands dominate the market in many fields.

Consequentially, promising organizations end up undercapitalized and undermanaged—effectively, stunted. For every Grameen Bank or BRAC, many others remain marginal for lack of rational financing. They are like Ferraris driving on mud tracks. Were social entrepreneurs able to access large pools of growth capital, they could do what competent businesspeople routinely do: create multiyear growth plans, raise the up-front capital to execute those plans, and evaluate their performance against pre-established goals.

It seems almost too prosaic to mention, but working from a plan can multiply an organization's effectiveness. Indeed, social entrepreneurs who participate in venture-planning competitions (typically sponsored by leading business schools) almost always find the experience valuable. Planning forces members of an organization to come together, set priorities, agree on the details of implementation, and turn vague intentions into time-bound goals. When people see how their contributions fit into the big picture, their motivation strengthens. Even clerical tasks take on more meaning when viewed as essential steps toward a shared goal.

Social organizations often neglect this process. One barrier is the shortage of people in this sector who have experience writing business plans. Another is the challenge of adapting the business-planning format to organizations that seek to cause social change rather than earn profits. Business plans are often full of revenue projections based on assumptions about market demand. For social entrepreneurs, planning must begin with a theory of change and an analysis of how an idea will spread, achieve impact, and influence others. Perhaps the biggest obstacle is a lack of belief in planning itself. The commonplace funding irregularities make planning seem more wishful than sensible. Changing the way we finance social change could produce greater clarity and more predictable successes.

How do social entrepreneurs finance organizations and enterprises?

Launching an organization is a process of recruiting funders, advisors, board members, and staffers, one by one. For young people, early support often comes from classmates, family friends, and professional relationships developed in internships or jobs. Early-stage social entrepreneurs often get a foot in the door of potential funders through recommendations from mentors or professors.

Only a few fellowship and prize programs specifically target social entrepreneurs. Together, they form an informal pipeline of support. For example, Youth Venture, YouthActionNet, and Do Something target youth; the Reynolds and Skoll foundations offer university fellowships; Echoing Green and the Draper Richards Foundation provide start-up financing; Ashoka supports social entrepreneurs from launch to maturity but targets most of its financial support at entrepreneurs whose organizations are poised to accelerate their growth or impact; New Profit Inc., the Skoll Foundation, the Jenesis Group, and Venture Philanthropy Partners provide growth funding. The Purpose Prize, created by Civic Ventures, directs support to social innovators over the age of sixty. Many other foundations provide support to social entrepreneurs without explicitly targeting them. For example, every member of Ashoka's Global Academy for Social Entrepreneurship has received support from the Ford Foundation at one point in their development.

Over the past thirty years, the resource landscape has exploded with a proliferation of financing options. Today, social organizations seeking support navigate a bewildering array of resources: community, family, corporate, and public foundations; social venture competitions; impact investors; Web-based intermediaries, such as GlobalGiving and CanadaHelps; funders who target a particular group, ranging from Hispanics to disabled people; and an array of social-business networks such as Net Impact and Social Venture Partners.

Inspired by the success of Web-based connectors, such as Kiva, MYC4, and DonorsChoose, many social entrepreneurs are also tapping support from large numbers of microcontributors. The Obama campaign used this tactic, redefining political fund-raising and breaking records. Moreover, people who begin with small financial contributions often end up devoting time and energy worth far more than their donations.

Ashoka identified this support-building technique in the 1990s as Fellows in many parts of the world reported success building decentralized bases of support from citizens (often in poor countries and without the benefit of the Internet). Social entrepreneurs tapped into the same yearning that Obama unearthed: the hunger to take part in real change. In countries that lacked cultures of philanthropy or volunteerism, they created bases of support by initiating competitions, cultural events, open houses, bartering arrangements, membership programs, and activist television and radio shows. Out of the assembled microcontributions of citizens they were able to build organizations capable of attacking problems on a major scale.

In Poland, for example, a group called the Workshop for All Beings organized citizens into a national network of "wildlife guardians," responsible for early detection of environmental threats. In Brazil, Doutores da Alegria places trained clowns and actors in hospitals where they bring laughter to children coping with serious illnesses. In India, street children trained by Childline as child protection advocates have responded to millions of emergency calls in more than 70 cities. In Burkina Faso, the Mouvement Burkinabé des Droits de l'Homme et des Peuples has enlisted tens of thousands of citizens to monitor human rights abuses. In Canada, the organization Roots of Empathy has brought thousands of mothers and babies into classrooms to teach empathy. In the United States, Bookshare has helped visually impaired people to work together to build the world's largest library of accessible books.

Over the past two decades, social entrepreneurs have also increasingly employed business strategies to address problems and generate revenues. In the mid 1980s, while Yunus and Abed were drawing attention to the potential of social enterprise in Bangladesh, Ed Skloot of New Ventures and Jerr Boschee of the National Center for Social Entrepreneurs were advancing this model for achieving impact and sustainability in the United States. The idea was taking root in other parts of the world, as well. By the early 1990s, more than a third of Ashoka fellows had launched earned-income ventures.

The spread of social enterprise was striking in the developing world, and as the pattern accelerated in the late 1990s, not everyone was pleased. In India, Brazil, Indonesia, Thailand, and South Africa, where many social activists were associated with leftist politics, many were apprehensive about experimenting with business models.

On the political left in general, the concern was that the introduction of business thinking in social organizations would damage their civic ethos. It would reduce human values to cost-benefit analyses. On the right, in keeping with Milton Friedman's dictum that "the business of business is business," the initial reaction was indifference. The belief was that businesses attempting to solve social problems would be uncompetitive.

Over the past decade, thinking and practice has evolved considerably, and these arguments are now being tested in thousands of enterprises worldwide. From the Grameen Bank and BRAC in Bangladesh, to ShoreBank in the United States, to the Self-Employed Women's Association in India, to the Population and Community Development Association in Thailand, many of the world's leading social organizations have achieved dramatic results through complementary nonprofit, business, and hybrid enterprises.

In *The Power of Unreasonable People*, John Elkington and Pamela Hartigan colorfully illustrate many ways that social entrepreneurs worldwide are addressing needs in health, education, technology, finance, environmental protection, and other areas through various organizational structures. In *Philanthrocapitalism*, Matthew Bishop and Michael Green show how the world's wealthiest business entrepreneurs are attacking problems by fusing business methods and philanthropy. Pierre Omidyar, the founder of eBay, for example, has created the Omidyar Network, a "philanthropic investment firm" that finances market-based efforts to catalyze economic and social changes. And Bill Gates directs some of his philanthropic efforts to champion a more "creative capitalism" to "stretch" markets so they better serve the poor.

Social enterprise promises to be a powerful change strategy. Profitable businesses grow quickly and attract imitators. A successful new business can shake up an industry almost overnight. Businesses are also compelled to listen to their clients in a way that charities are not. The shift from "beneficiaries" to "customers" isn't only a shift from "free" to "fee." When done well, it can reorient the focus of an organization from its own needs to the needs of its clients.

To be sure, many businesses are poorly managed, and many social goods do not lend themselves to market approaches. In coming years, perhaps entrepreneurs will devise business models to provide affordable health insurance, quality education, or organic food to poor inner-city families. But so far, it hasn't happened. In these areas, it currently seems more likely that people will create new enterprises that break even, earn a token profit, or require a partial subsidy.

Jed Emerson coined the term "blended value" to describe the commingling of social and financial objectives. As more organizations work in this gray area, they will require new kinds of financing, especially financing that crosses the borders between philanthropy, business, and the public sector. Social entrepreneurship used to operate in a binary world of pure grant making (–100 percent returns) and pure market investing (+5 percent returns, or better). This omitted a wide range of investment opportunities. Today, as a result of initiatives such as Ashoka's Social Financial Services program, the Acumen Fund Investor Gatherings, the Social Capital Markets (SOCAP) conferences, the South Asia Social Enterprise and Investment Forum, the Aspen Network of Development Entrepreneurs, and the Global Impact Investing Network, entrepreneurs and investors are learning how to combine the full spectrum of financing instruments, which include grants, equity, soft loans, and commercial debt, to maximize social impact. Good Capital, Gray Matters Capital, KL Felicitas Foundation, Investors' Circle, Intellecap, Bridges Ventures, and the Deutsche Bank Eye Fund are examples of blended-value or "impact investors" that target social businesses.

In their 2009 report, *Investing for Social and Environmental Impact*, Jessica Freireich and Katherine Fulton of the Monitor Institute note that impact investing is moving from the "periphery" to the "core of mainstream financial institutions," with major growth since 2001 in funds to promote clean technology, health care, microfinance, and small-business development, among other areas. (Microfinance is now regularly funded by a combination of philanthropy, government money, impact investment, and market capital.) Freireich and Fulton argue that for impact investing to thrive, a new industry will have to emerge to supply such missing pieces as metrics to evaluate success, new financial products, and social stock exchanges. New developments in the latter area include Brazil's Environmental and Social Investment Exchange (BVS&A), an initiative of Bovespa, the São Paulo Stock Exchange, the South African Social Investment Exchange (SASIX), and the newly created Impact Investment Exchange Asia (IIX Asia), which has received support from the Singapore government, the Asian Development Bank and the Rockefeller Foundation.

Philanthropy is also being redeployed to harness traditional market mechanisms to produce social benefits. For
example, Endeavor is a nonprofit organization that supports
for-profit entrepreneurs in the developing world, an idea that
drew blank stares when it was launched in 1997. The organization provides credibility and network support to entrepreneurs in countries where they face hurdles getting started; it
measures success based on the number and quality of jobs
that its entrepreneurs create. The Acumen Fund, which calls
itself a nonprofit venture capital firm, pools grants and makes
loans and equity investments in companies that deliver health
care, water, housing, and energy to underserved markets in
developing countries. Some of the most promising delivery
systems for many basic needs are turning out to be market-
based.

Currently, these crossover institutions are poorly understood. We lack tools to assess risk and measure social impact,
which makes it difficult for investment markets to expand.
For-profit investors get scared off when they hear that an organization is seeking social returns, and grant makers become
worried when they hear applicants talk about profits, though
often with good reason, as the lines between social and
commercial enterprises are not always clear.

One new development that may help is the establishment of
a legal category now recognized by several U.S. states: a low-
profit limited liability company, or "L3C," which is intended
to simplify the process by which foundations can invest in
social-purpose businesses while complying with Internal
Revenue Service rules. (In the United Kingdom, the rough
equivalent is the Community Interest Company, or CIC.)
Neither designation currently offers preferable tax treatment,
but that would be a logical next step.

The question of how to finance and build effective social change organizations gets to a deeper set of challenges: determining which legal structures and organizational formats are best suited to different kinds of problems. This is not merely a question of determining whether something should be handled through a business, social, or governmental entity, or financed by investment, philanthropy, or tax dollars.

Arguments between all-or-nothing pro-market and pro-government ideologues still fill up our political discourse, but they are fast becoming anachronisms. Stark distinctions between for-profit, nonprofit and governmental organizations no longer serve society's needs. As people and capital begin to move more fluidly across the old sector boundaries, we are likely to break free of mindsets that limit our ability to imagine solutions.

Can the field attract and cultivate talented workers?

Social entrepreneurs attack big problems with limited resources. The field is young, and many of its institutions are in their formative stages. While conventional entrepreneurs can build upon well-established business models, social entrepreneurs often forge ahead without road maps. For these reasons, social entrepreneurship is currently more talent-intensive than ordinary business, and the jobs are more open-ended.

Presently, social entrepreneurs have to recruit talent without being able to offer compensation on a par with business. They succeed instead by inspiring people and offering meaningful work. Successful social entrepreneurs go to great lengths to help people see how their abilities might be channeled to bring significant change. Some, like Bill Drayton, prioritize this above all else.

Drayton describes social entrepreneurs as "mass recruiters" for building new ideas. However, most of this recruitment takes place informally. The social sector does not yet have sophisticated systems to nurture talent. Teach For America, the only social-change organization that regularly recruits on top college campuses alongside investment banks and consulting firms, has been amazingly successful redirecting talent into public education. Its approach is exemplary. One of its tactics is to make the process competitive and prestigious. Another is to enlist alumni to tell stories about transformative moments in their classrooms. Yet another is to frame the job as a challenge, similar to an Outward Bound or Peace Corps experience. Finally, candidates are inspired to join a community of people who are fighting for justice, many of whom will become lifelong friends.

In their book *The Charismatic Organization*, Shirley Sagawa and Deb Jospin show how organizations, like individuals, take on personalities. Charismatic groups are those that are driven by values, open to experimentation, focused on results, good at communication, and genuinely appreciative of people. They develop vibrant cultures that act like magnets for staff, volunteers, board members, and other partners. However, what draws people to a "charismatic organization" may not keep them there. Retaining talent is especially hard in the social sector because of the financial inhibitors to growth. Organizations need to grow so they can offer progressively interesting and challenging work. Rational financing and talent recruitment therefore go hand in hand.

At present, cultural shifts seem to be working in favor of social entrepreneurs. In recent years, university professors across the United States and Canada have observed that, while students of the past were interested in work that offered longevity and stability, today's students seek work-life balance and meaning. The most popular course at Harvard teaches students how to be happy, reminding them that the answer doesn't lie chiefly in financial success but in meaningful work, good relationships, time for reflection, and the cultivation of gratitude.

As a mark of interest in the field, the recent ratio of applications to positions at esteemed social change organizations such as Bridgespan, the Acumen Fund, or Endeavor has been roughly 100 to 1. In 2008, the Reynolds Program for Social Entrepreneurship at NYU received more than 1,000 applications for 14 fellowships. Social enterprise clubs at leading business schools are generally among the most popular on campus.

On the other end of the age spectrum, Civic Ventures, which launched the Purpose Prize in 2006 to recognize social innovators who are over the age of 60, has received thousands of nominations, revealing a hidden landscape of people pursuing service-oriented encore careers—a movement that may transform retirement for baby boomers. Many of these people say that their "encores" are the most satisfying work they have ever done.

The appeal of work with meaning extends into the heart of the corporate world. We have noted the rise of impact investing. When J.P. Morgan created a social sector finance unit in 2007, more than a thousand bank employees sent in resumes, explaining their interest in transferring to the unit or their willingness to contribute time to help.

Still, the lure of corporate success remains strong. Student debt and family and peer expectations make it difficult to pass up lucrative job offers. In the spring of 2008, the *Harvard Crimson* surveyed 600 seniors about their career plans. Only 20 percent considered finance, business, or management consulting to be "dream jobs," but 40 percent planned to work in those areas. One in four seniors said their dream would be to work in the arts or public service, but only one in eight planned to pursue those routes. The market crash has changed the job calculus in the short run. Harvard's Social Enterprise Conference 2009 was standing room only. Students indicated that the evaporation of high-paying jobs made it easier to choose work they cared about.

Leaders of social organizations have only recently come to recognize that they can compete head to head for talent with businesses by offering salaries that, while not commensurate, are tolerable. In the past, the implicit assumption was that people either chose money or meaning. Social-sector salaries were often set so much lower than corporate salaries that, for people on the fence, the cost of choosing a "meaningful" career was too high. Even those content to earn less than their market price want to be reasonably valued. As the recent market crisis has demonstrated, people may not be willing to accept a 60 percent pay cut, but they may be willing to accept one of 30 percent. In the future, it will be important to find out where the scale tips or, in the language of economics, what is social entrepreneurship's income elasticity.

Salaries have come up in the citizen sector. Leaders in the field often earn incomes between $100,000 and $200,000, and occasionally higher. Historically, foundations and the media have looked askance at these higher compensation levels. Social rating agencies compare overhead levels with total program costs—and draw attention to groups where the ratio is above 20 percent. Taken alone, though, these crude measures are meaningless and can be damaging. They make groups that pay higher salaries appear less efficient, and even less ethical, without providing meaningful information about the organizations' impact.

In the decades ahead, the gap in compensation will likely narrow further, though the market crisis will of course reduce foundation expenditures in the near term. It's clear that many of the institutions that need to be built will require an influx of talent from business, finance, medicine, law, engineering, and other fields where salary expectations are higher. New talent recruitment firms like Bridgestar, Commongood Careers, and On-Ramps are already serving the growing market for blended careers. People will still earn less for the privilege of doing meaningful work, but the drop won't be as jarring as it has been in the past. And of course, entrepreneurs who are successful at building social enterprises will prosper, though many will opt to cap returns to preserve the centrality of their missions.

Finally, social entrepreneurs need to do more to cultivate their own talent gardens. Organizations that seek to advance change in the world must also create internal spaces for people to discover their potential through experimentation. In practice, this means celebrating people who take initiative, even when their ideas don't work. Encouraging and integrating the ambitions of many self-starters is a complex management job and can lead to internal tension. But it is a microcosm of the global challenge we face: building a world of active citizens.

How do social entrepreneurs evaluate their impact?

As mentioned, social entrepreneurship is characterized by a rigorous focus on results, traditionally a weak spot for social programs. Consider after-school education. The federal government spends billions annually on after-school programs to assist young children who perform below grade level, especially in reading and math. Unfortunately, large-scale studies have found that most of these programs fail to boost student achievement.

But not all of them do. Some groups outperform others by a big margin, and the ones that do closely monitor their own performance. One such organization, BELL (Building Educated Leaders for Life), which uses a proven curriculum and has an award-winning training program for its instructors, has demonstrated substantial gains in students' math and reading skills. Not only can BELL tell you how far its students have advanced during the school year, but it can tell you, week by week, how they are progressing. When a student falls off pace, red flags go up, and the organization does its best to remedy the situation. Most of BELL's competitors could tell you how many students attended their programs and the number of hours each sat in class, but they can't tell you what the children learned.

BELL receives no preferences from the government over other approved "service providers," most of which pay less attention to quality. The organization doesn't get paid more, and it doesn't receive priority access in schools where the need is greatest. In a more sensible world, BELL's success would be recognized, rewarded, and copied. But, as previously mentioned, in the social arena, mediocrity frequently trumps excellence—a situation that many social entrepreneurs and their funders are working to change.

Measuring test scores on a few core subjects is just one way to gauge educational results—and a limited one at that. Albert Einstein hung a sign in his office that read: "Not everything that counts can be counted, and not everything that can be counted counts." Nowhere is this saying more true than in the social sector, where attempts to measure results are notoriously difficult.

In business, you can assess the financial performance of a company, whether it sells coffee or cars, by distilling its results down to return on investment (ROI). But consider the example of an organization like Playworks, which teaches children how to play well in teams, govern their impulses, and resolve conflicts in the schoolyard. Some psychologists argue that these indications of emotional intelligence are better predictors of life success than academic achievement. Nonetheless, this dimension of education is largely ignored because it is so difficult to measure.

Measuring long-term results in the social sector is even more difficult. At the highest levels, social entrepreneurs seek to change attitudes toward such issues as disability, global warming, or gay marriage. Attitudinal changes on the societal level usually unfold over decades, so it is nearly impossible to determine how and why they changed. And within the sector, the challenge of comparison is daunting. It seems impossible to prioritize between early childhood education or college access, or between protecting rain forests, fisheries, or grasslands.

Because these questions are so difficult, funders have often sidestepped them, making decisions based on anecdotal evidence, personal preference, or political exigency. However, in recent years funders have begun applying more systematic techniques to assess their grantees' progress against a range of self-determined goals. New Profit Inc., which supports social entrepreneurs with growth funding, helps its "portfolio" members implement a performance management tool called the Balanced Scorecard, created by Harvard Business School Professor Robert Kaplan. The Edna McConnell Clark, Robert Wood Johnson, and William and Flora Hewlett foundations are among the larger foundations that have invested considerable resources in performance tracking. Without external pressure from funders, social organizations have often been content to assess their own performance in the crudest of ways: by the growth of their budgets or number of people "served." Thus, an ineffective after-school program can claim success by wasting the time of more children each year.

The weakness of these measures was famously highlighted by the Nature Conservancy fifteen years ago. For years, the conservancy had measured its success based on dollars raised and land area protected ("bucks and acres"). But in the 1990s, as these figures rose so did species extinction rates—even in protected areas. The recognition forced the organization to reappraise its performance evaluation. It spent years developing dozens of new metrics to evaluate biodiversity health and the abatement of extinction threats. The process revolutionized the way decisions were made at all levels of the organization. The lesson was that what you count determines what you do. So it's important to count the right things.

This thinking animates the field of socially responsible investing, which directs resources to companies that pursue a "triple bottom line," a term coined by John Elkington, which refers to social, environmental, and financial performance. In social entrepreneurship, creative efforts to translate impact into dollar terms have focused not on fund-raising, but on outcomes that are directly linked to an organization's purpose. Jed Emerson and the Roberts Enterprise Development Fund led the way in the 1990s developing tools to calculate a "social return on investment" (SROI). Using its framework, for example, a welfare-to-work program would estimate the reductions in government spending and increases in tax payments directly attributable to its successes. Dividing benefits by costs gives you the social return, an especially useful tool for programs that save the government money.

In recent years, the Washington State Institute for Public Policy has applied this thinking at the state level, calculating the expected returns of crime prevention programs. (The net present value of providing family therapy to one youth on probation is $50,000.) The problem is that long-term savings, even when valued in present dollars, continue to have limited appeal to lawmakers who need to win reelection every two years.

In their report *Breakthroughs in Shared Measurement and Social Impact*, Mark Kramer, Marcie Parkhurst and Lalitha Vaidyanathan describe several new Web-based systems that evaluate the performance of social enterprises. They contend that these models foreshadow "profound changes in the vision and effectiveness" of the social sector. Two such efforts are the Global Impact Investing Network's "Impact Reporting and Investment Standards" (IRIS), developed by the Rockefeller Foundation, and supported by Deloitte Consulting and Price-Waterhouse Coopers, and the Pulse portfolio management system, spearheaded by the Acumen Fund, with support from Google, and the Skoll, Kellogg, Lodestar and Salesforce.com foundations. The Pulse system assesses the financial, operating, social, and environmental performance of social enterprises using a blend of individualized reporting and common metrics (measurement tools). The goal is to simplify the decision making for investors who are willing to accept lower financial returns for higher social impact. In *Simple Measures for Social Enterprise*, Brian Trelstad, who leads Acumen's efforts developing Pulse (and who describes himself as a cross between a merchant and a missionary), notes that a sector-wide solution to the challenge of evaluating social investments is within reach. The toughest part, he says, will be getting institutions to collaborate and share information.

If successful, standards, accreditors, and even social-enterprise rating agencies may follow, which will help protect the field from conventional investments being falsely promoted as impact investments.

Organizations pursuing long-term impact often assess their progress against a theory of change. Consider again Teach For America, which recruits college graduates to serve in two-year teaching stints in public schools that are located in low-income communities. Teach For America's goal is to ensure that all children receive a good education. To do that, it must attack problems that were set in motion by the middle-class migration to the suburbs after World War II, which left minority areas deprived of strong tax bases and political influence, and resulted in decades of school decline.

Teach For America doesn't expect to solve these problems by placing a few thousand teachers each year. Its strategy is to seed educational institutions at all levels with leaders from the nation's top colleges who appreciate today's educational challenges and are committed to reform. Accordingly, the organization measures success by the number of alumni who assume leadership positions in public education.

All successful organizations have preferred metrics. For Ashoka, it's the percentage of fellows whose work has shifted patterns in their fields. For the Grameen Bank, it's the percentage of borrowers who have risen out of poverty. Translating a social change into a meaningful number is an artful task. Measuring reductions in poverty is not as straightforward as looking at changes in income levels. Poverty has objective and subjective dimensions. Recognizing this, the Grameen Bank developed a metric based on feedback from villagers to determine when a family should be deemed nonpoor. The metric takes into account whether a family has a tin roof, bedding, clothing and mosquito nets, access to safe drinking water and a sanitary latrine, all children attending school, and adequate food, even in months preceding harvests.

Even these finely tuned measures miss much of the story. Because of the spread of microfinance in Bangladesh, girls attend school at higher rates than in the past. The most consistent global predictor of the well-being of a society is women's educational attainment. This ancillary benefit of microfinance is difficult to assess but it may have the most far-reaching impact of all.

Finally, Einstein cautioned against relying too much on knowledge at the expense of feeling. "We must take care not to make intellect our god," he asserted. "It has, of course, powerful muscles, but no personality. It cannot rule, only serve." Just as it takes two eyes set apart to see the world in three dimensions, it is only by combining data and storytelling, and by appealing to reason and emotion, that social entrepreneurs convey the true impact of their work. It's one thing to talk about an increase in reading scores and quite another to describe the delight in the eyes of a young girl who reads her first sentence. Orchestra conductor and music educator Benjamin Zander assesses his success by the sparkle in the eyes of people in his audiences as he helps them to discover the pleasures of classical music. His evaluation is immediate, objective, and powerful. It counts, but it cannot be counted.

What is the difference between scale and impact?

Jeffrey Hollender, the founder of Seventh Generation, a $100 million manufacturer that pioneered green household cleaning products, served as an unpaid advisor to Wal-Mart to help the massive retailer shift to environmentally sustainable products. In doing so, Hollender encouraged the world's biggest corporation to compete with his own firm. Many businesspeople would consider this unwise. But Hollender knows that Wal-Mart has far more power to safeguard the environment than Seventh Generation does. At the highest level, success for a social entrepreneur is not about building the biggest or best organization in the field. It is about changing the field.

Most research that focuses on the issue of scale focuses on organizational scale and the question of how to finance and manage growing institutions. To be sure, this is a critical area of inquiry: the social sector has lots of great ideas but few great institutions. But it's important to distinguish organizational scale and scale of impact. The two do not necessarily go hand in hand.

In 1988, Alan Khazei and Michael Brown founded City Year to demonstrate how national service programs—nonmilitary, structured opportunities for citizens to serve—could transform society. At the time, national service was an idea that had been championed by policy makers and philosophers for more than a century, but it had never gained political traction. The idea needed to be made attractive to policy makers and to the public.

City Year connected the energy and creativity of urban youth with social needs. Its corps members—proud in their distinctive red, yellow, and black jackets and inculcated in a culture of respect, team spirit, and discipline—became charismatic ambassadors for national service. Visits to City Year made such a powerful impression on Bill Clinton during his 1992 presidential campaign that he credited the program with inspiring his vision for AmeriCorps, the federal program that has mobilized more than 600,000 volunteers.

The passage of the Edward M. Kennedy Serve America Act, which President Obama signed into law in April 2009, will triple the reach of AmeriCorps and expand service opportunities for older Americans. The legislation would almost certainly not exist if not for City Year's pioneering efforts, the organization's willingness to share its knowledge, and more than twenty years of advocacy led by Khazei and Brown.

City Year was a small organization in the early 1990s. Its outsize impact came not through its direct reach but through its influence. In *Forces for Good*, Leslie Crutchfield and Heather McLeod Grant show that organizations that achieve far-reaching impact think well beyond their own institutional boundaries. They leverage power by documenting and sharing their work and building networks, coalitions, alliances, and movements to shape social norms and policies.

Of course, size and influence do often go together. But while most organizations give considerable thought to the question of how to scale up directly, many fail to consider how to effect change beyond their immediate reach. The most dynamic groups are the ones that focus extensively on this challenge.

When an organization is effective, people naturally ask whether it is sustainable. Typically, the answer hinges on its ability to raise funds to keep going year after year. Like scale, the idea of sustainability can be considered in two ways: the sustainability of an institution and the sustainability of ideas or values. The way we speak about sustainability usually refers to individual institutions. This is limiting. It's like speaking about the lives of trees rather than the lives of forests. Both are important, but just as trees fall and are absorbed into the ground, institutions go through cycles of growth and decay. Some find ways to renew themselves; some die off. In thinking about sustainability, it is key to focus on the forests.

There was once a time when the future of microfinance was contingent on the fortunes of the Grameen Bank. Today, microfinance is no longer dependent on any one institution. No one is "too big to fail." If the Grameen Bank collapsed, its borrowers and staff would certainly suffer. But in time, other microlenders would absorb them. Seeds have spread and a forest has grown. The vitality of an idea, widely understood and accepted, keeps it alive. Significant credit for this change must go to Sam Daley-Harris, the social entrepreneur behind the Microcredit Summit Campaign, which helped thousands of independent organizations coalesce into a global movement that achieved audacious goals in less than a decade.

People will continue to create newer and better microfinance organizations into the future because they know they *can* do it, they know *how* to do it, and they know *why* it is worth their effort. A field is truly sustainable when its institutions can be readily renewed and improved upon.

What's stopping social change?

In *The Wealth of Nations*, Adam Smith wrote that the "greatest improvement in the productive powers of society" came from the "division of labor." Smith used the example of a small pin factory to show that if instead of making whole pins, each worker specialized on a narrow aspect of production, and they all later combined their efforts, they could produce tens of thousands of pins in a day, rather than a few hundred.

Smith's insight provided the theoretical framework for the industrial revolution. During the early twentieth century, the idea became widely applied in industry after Frederick Winslow Taylor published *The Principles of Scientific Management*, which sought to maximize productive efficiency through narrow "task allocation" and "enforced standardization of methods." However, the division of labor influenced far more than factory assembly lines; over time, the principle took hold across society. As specialization and atomization became the norm, people in different industries, professions, and sectors moved farther apart.

Today, for example, the bridges that link businesses, social organizations, and government agencies remain narrow and undertraveled. Government agencies are themselves "stove-piped" and rarely interact. (The 9/11 Commission described the absence of "government-wide information sharing" as a serious threat to national security.)

Without specialization, of course, we wouldn't have affordable computers, life-saving vaccines, or deep understandings of psychology or aeronautics. Nor would we have achieved the widespread prosperity enjoyed in industrialized societies. At the same time, the institutional and conceptual barriers that separate fields, industries, and sectors make it difficult to construct whole solutions.

It is widely understood that health problems among the poor are frequently caused or triggered by social conditions: damp, dirty, or cockroach-infested housing, or lack of money to pay for nutritious food, medicine or heating fuel. American hospitals in poor areas regularly treat children for diabetes, asthma, lung infections, and malnutrition and then discharge the kids without doing anything to stem the root causes of their illnesses. Overworked social workers have little time to focus on anything but the most serious cases of abuse and neglect.

The U.S. health system is organized around individualized care. A poor mother trying to assist a child with asthma might need to connect, separately, with a pediatrician, a nutritionist, an allergist, a physiotherapist, a health insurance specialist, a social worker, a housing advocate, an exterminator, a school nurse, a gym instructor, and perhaps even a pollution inspector from the Environmental Protection Agency (and possibly all through a translator). Pieces of the solution are so scattered that assembling them can be an overwhelming challenge.

It makes no sense to attack many social problems in piecemeal fashion. For example, social service workers contend that the single best way to improve health outcomes in a low-income community would be to improve access to decent low-cost housing. Yet our health and housing systems run in parallel, with few connecting bridges. One innovative organization, Project Health, deploys student volunteers in hospital units to help doctors integrate a social diagnosis into routine medical care. Similarly, some health centers, like the Mayo Clinic, practice collaborative medicine, allowing doctors and other health workers to pool their patient knowledge. They achieve high-quality care at low cost. But Project Health and the Mayo Clinic are exceptions to the rule.

The division of labor leads to absurdities when applied to human needs. Thus we build old-age facilities where everyone is older than 75. It is easier to deliver assistive services in these places, but they don't facilitate the cross-generational relationships that are vital to health and happiness. We sequester adolescent children from older and younger students. We remove disabled people from mainstream society. Old age homes, middle schools, and institutions for the disabled treat people as if they were pins, to be processed as efficiently as possible. Today we consider these structures to be normal, but as Gandhi said, we shouldn't confuse what is habitual with what is normal.

In societies divided into specialized arenas, career paths are vertical, not horizontal, so preexisting beliefs within fields or industries tend to be reinforced rather than questioned. People are less likely to develop relationships that challenge their world-views or expand their empathy and understanding for other groups. They are also more likely to have significant blind spots. It is an intolerable contradiction that the health sector is the largest source of dioxins and mercury in our food supply and environment. A hospital CEO may have no clue how his or her purchasing or waste-disposal decisions spread harmful toxins. Similarly, an environmentalist might advocate for stronger conservation laws without appreciating the effect of those policies on people's livelihoods. And law enforcement agencies focus on punishing individual offenders, but rarely take the critical step of engaging their families in the process of rehabilitation.

In the United States and Canada today, patterns of separation extend to whole communities. A child growing up in the suburbs may reach college without once encountering a poor person in the flesh. When too many people across society have difficulty taking the perspective of others, polarization and political stagnation result.

Innovation and change demand the recombination of knowledge—new recipes, not just more cooking. In a society oriented around specialization, where knowledge is fragmented, entrepreneurs play critical integrating roles. Entrepreneurship is a fusion process. Steve Jobs didn't develop the processors, graphic interface, or early spreadsheet applications that made home computing easy, affordable, and useful. But he was the one who brought the pieces together.

Social entrepreneurs are creative combiners, carving out spaces in society to foster whole solutions. If they "specialize" in anything, it is bringing people together who wouldn't coalesce naturally. Eboo Patel created the Interfaith Youth Core, based in Chicago, to bring together young people from different faiths to collaborate on solving social problems. Patel's model has demonstrated a way to build trust, respect, and collegiality in the post 9/11 world. Gerald Chertavian spent years as a Big Brother mentor for low-income youths while working on Wall Street. From his dual vantage point, he was able to understand what it would take to connect these two groups. His organization, Year Up, successfully prepares urban youths for corporate careers.

Today, we are witnessing many promising developments along these collaborative lines. Examples include the emergence of business schools that integrate sustainability in every course, and multidisciplinary programs in social entrepreneurship that draw students from a variety of faculties. We've seen a rise in popularity of interdisciplinary conferences—TED, PopTech, Good Experience Live, Aspen Ideas Festival—which have played roles linking people from different sectors and fields. The World Economic Forum has opened itself modestly to social entrepreneurs. The action-oriented Clinton Global Initiative brings together business leaders, philanthropists, policy makers, and social innovators and gives the latter group a prominent role. Now President Obama has created an Office of Social Innovation in the White House which is aimed at integrating the insights of social entrepreneurs into high-level policy making.

Perhaps the nation's preeminent social integrator is Geoffrey Canada, founder of the Harlem Children's Zone. Teachers know that children who come to school hungry and exhausted will have trouble learning. Canada recognized that to address the interrelated social problems in a large area of Harlem, he would have to find ways to provide assistance in many areas at once: parenting skills, early-childhood and K-12 education, college access, health and fitness, community organization, and political representation. The Harlem Children's Zone is considered one of the most important social experiments in the United States. Its early success demonstrates that when it comes to solving social problems, the integration of labor is likely the way forward.

III

ENVISIONING AN INNOVATING SOCIETY

How is social entrepreneurship changing minds?

In describing the causes of poverty, Muhammad Yunus has often compared a poor person to a bonsai tree. The seed of a bonsai has the potential to grow into a full-size tree, but, planted in a tiny pot, its growth is stunted. To Yunus, a person deprived of education or opportunity is like a bonsai. The constraint isn't the seed, it's the pot. Yunus has noted that his "greatest challenge" has been getting this point across: changing mindsets about the poor, about financial institutions, about the nature of capitalism itself, which all stunt the growth of millions. "Mindsets play strange tricks on us," he says. "We see things the way our minds have instructed our eyes to see."

The most important mindset shift that social entrepreneurs are working to effect today is convincing people that the world's toughest problems can be solved. In the United States, for example, over the past forty years, confidence in many social institutions, including government, religion, medicine, law, banking, public education, and journalism, has plummeted. In this context, organizations like the Grameen Bank, BRAC, Ashoka, Echoing Green, Teach For America, City Year, the Harlem Children's Zone and Youth Villages—to cite just a few examples—demonstrate new possibilities and may have the potential to renew hope and optimism at a societal level.

Social entrepreneurs also work to shift mindsets about what is possible at the individual level. Many have found ways to unleash human potential among individuals who have historically been viewed as incompetent, expendable, or beyond rehabilitation.

In India, for example, Childline enlists street kids as the front lines of a national child protection network. In Canada, the Planned Lifetime Advocacy Network has shown that disabled people who are welcomed as full community participants enrich others' lives in unforeseeable ways. In the United States, Peace Games trains fifth graders in urban elementary schools to be "peace builders" who teach younger students how to resolve conflicts in lunchrooms and in the schoolyard. According to principals, the peace builders transform school culture, making it more conducive for learning. Whether they are prison inmates, illiterate peasants, ten-year-olds, or seventy-year-olds, we undervalue people when we define them by their perceived deficits.

Innovators flip the lens: they look for strengths to build upon. In so doing, they expose myths about the creativity, resilience, and moral agency of people who are poor, illiterate, disabled, drug addicted, incarcerated, or simply outside the age range we think of as productive years. They have demonstrated that institutions which assume that most people are competent and honest regularly outperform those which expect the worst.

In *The Ecology of Commerce*, Paul Hawken asserted that in every area of our economy we will have to find ways of accomplishing twice as much, with half the resources. To do so, we'll have to approach our challenges with what Buddhists call "beginner's mind"—a way of thinking that is open, alert, and free of dogma and what Thorstein Veblen called "trained incapacity." We have many examples to guide and inspire us today. Before microfinance came along, for example, bankers assumed that loans had to be managed one-on-one and secured with collateral, two stipulations that excluded the poor. And before Paul Farmer, Jim Yong Kim, and their colleagues in Partners in Health developed and promoted Directly Observed Therapy for multidrug-resistant tuberculosis and HIV/AIDS, few believed that these diseases could be successfully managed among the poor in developing countries.

Today, networks of schools founded by social entrepreneurs in the United States, like Green Dot Public Schools, Uncommon Schools, and the Knowledge Is Power Program (KIPP), are getting impressive—and sometimes amazing—results with disadvantaged students by modifying the structure of the school day and year, providing extensive support to teachers, engaging families, and employing a teaching model that stresses character education and high levels of class participation. Businesses are increasingly integrating social, financial, and environmental performance goals. And new health care models are improving outcomes and lowering costs by giving more discretion to nurses, offering patients simplified decision aids, and helping doctors to incorporate the best available evidence in their treatments.

All these changes have come about because people who were dissatisfied with the status quo sought alternatives to the old approaches. And just as X-rays and penicillin were discovered by scientists who were looking for other things, the social innovators behind these changes didn't always know where they were heading. They experimented, observed, and adjusted. Mike Feinberg and Dave Levin, the founders of the KIPP schools, spent years improvising their teaching approach, picking and choosing elements from educators they admired and figuring out how to engage students and their families.

People who see beyond existing frameworks have three qualities that stand out. The first is a passionate interest in simple, even seemingly childish, questions, such as: Why *can't* we extend loans to villagers? Or: Why *won't* the students pay attention in class? The second is a practice of questioning one's own, and society's, assumptions, and reflecting on how they play out in institutions: *How do beliefs about inner-city children influence the way schools teach them*? And the third is a persistence of looking and a determination to go to the source—in this case, the villagers, the students, or their parents—to gain a solid understanding of the problems at hand.

In the previous section we described how institutional and conceptual barriers impede problem solving and how social entrepreneurs play the integrating role. They also play an important role building institutions that help people understand the interdependent nature of global society.

Americans exalt self-reliance. It takes a system breakdown—a blackout or a tainted meat recall—to remind us that we depend on others every day and that others depend on us. Each day we all make small decisions that ripple out into the world in unforeseeable ways—everything from how we speak to our children, to what we choose to eat, to how we get around, to what products we opt to buy and how we dispose of them. One of the critical roles of the environmental movement over the past thirty years—from Earth Day to treehugger. com—has been to help people understand the relationship between individual behavior and large-scale environmental problems, such as smog, river contamination, deforestation, species extinction, and global warming.

The psychologist Abraham Maslow defined a hierarchy of human needs that progress from survival to spiritual self-actualization. Philosopher Ken Wilber has argued that societies pass through analogous stages of consciousness, and, as they do, their values reflect a progressive appreciation of the integral nature of the world. Simply put, our thinking moves from "me" to "us" and, eventually, to "all of us." The Pew Charitable Trusts has funded global polls that identify growing numbers of people worldwide who identify as "global citizens." Paul Ray and Sherry Anderson, coauthors of the book *The Cultural Creatives*, report that 50 million people in the United States and 90 million in Europe share common values and regard the world as a single interwoven society and ecosystem.

In *Nonzero: The Logic of Human Destiny*, Robert Wright asserts that this mindset shift is a necessary evolutionary adaptation. He argues that the world has no choice but to move progressively from what he calls "zero-sum" to "non-zero-sum" thinking: from a model of interaction in which one party's win is another's loss to a model in which all parties benefit. The nature of today's threats—from greenhouse gases to disease epidemics to economic crises—require coordinated global solutions. In a world where small actors, aided by technology, can destabilize nation states, the powerful can no longer ignore those presumed to be weak.

We are bound up in each other's fate, Wright demonstrates, and many social entrepreneurs are building institutions that reflect this fact. The fair trade movement, for example, has helped consumers understand the economic and environmental ramifications of the coffee they drink and the T-shirts they wear on the lives of farmers or garment workers half a world away. The Marine Stewardship Council has helped thousands of people involved in the fishing and seafood industries, as well as retailers and consumers, understand how they can take action to preserve the health of ocean life.

Groups such as Social Accountability International have helped businesspeople in industrialized countries, such as buyers or designers for large clothing chains, to understand the effects of their decisions. A late-season style change, ordered by a Manhattan-based designer, may require thousands of Chinese factory employees to work overtime for weeks to meet a compressed deadline. Today, that designer can weigh the benefits and the human costs before making the decision. Groups like RugMark International and Verité let consumers know when products are tainted by child slavery, illegal child labor, or other human rights violations. Increasingly, manufacturers and retailers are offering consumers "supply chain transparency" or "traceability" through codes that provide information about product origins.

Gandhi famously said that we must "be the change" we wish to see in the world. And Archbishop Desmond Tutu has spoken about the African ethical concept of "ubuntu," which stresses the interconnectedness of humanity. "A person is a person through other persons," Tutu has said. "We think of ourselves far too frequently as just individuals, separated from one another," he explains. "[W]hat you do affects the whole world."

These ideas are more easily understood at the personal rather than at the global level, even if they are always difficult to apply consistently. If we want to live in a more peaceful world, it is easy to understand that we should try to engage peacefully with our families, friends, and colleagues. Applying this idea at the global level is complicated. Even Gandhi failed to take into account how his words would hurt poor textile workers in England when he asked Indians to burn their foreign-made clothes and wear only local hand-woven cloth. To consider all the effects of our actions on people and the environment is impossible.

Each effort and action, however, strengthens a sense of connection, builds empathy, and reminds us that our lives are contingent on others. Collectively, these fragments build support for larger structural changes. The creation of the International Criminal Court, for example, or the Convention on the Rights of the Child, are compacts that represent (near) global aspirations to protect and ensure the dignity of each life.

How could schools nurture social innovators?

In their book *The Scientist in the Crib*, authors Alison Gopnik, Andrew N. Meltzoff, and Patricia K. Kuhl observe that babies and toddlers from their earliest years "think, draw conclusions, make predictions, look for explanations, and even do experiments." Children know far more about the world than adults imagine, and they seek to understand everything they touch and taste. During their first two years, they make extraordinary intellectual leaps.

For most children, intellectual development slows dramatically within a few years. By the time they are in grade school, children have lost much of the curiosity and resourcefulness that a few years earlier made them incomparable explorers. As the noted educator Eleanor Duckworth explains in her book *The Having of Wonderful Ideas*, once children enroll in school, their natural enthusiasm and inquisitiveness becomes subordinated to the needs of adults enlisted to teach them. A young child who breaks something to see what it looks like inside, or asks a question that is socially embarrassing, or wants to discover how it feels to wear shoes on the wrong feet, will often be met with a discouraging glance or tone from an adult. Duckworth contends that many valid intellectual pursuits by children are dismissed by adults as trivial, unacceptable, or inconvenient. She argues that educators should encourage and structure moments when children can have their own ideas and feel good for having them. Only if children honestly believe their ideas are valuable will they develop the interest, ability, and self-confidence to be lifelong learners and doers. Duckworth adds, "Having confidence in one's ideas does not mean 'I know my ideas are right'; it means 'I am willing to try out my ideas.'"

The heart of social entrepreneurship is a willingness to try out ideas that are helpful to others. Social entrepreneurs are action researchers: they learn primarily through experimentation, not just by relying on theory. They approach the world the way a tinkerer approaches a broken clock. Educating young people to think and behave this way is different from helping them to acquire knowledge. Presenting the educational challenge in this light exposes the limitations of standardized tests.

Given the way the world is changing, more people are going to have to improvise large stretches of their careers, responding to shifting needs and opportunities. Success may hinge less on what you know than on how well you learn new things, spot patterns, take initiative, and work with others. The development of empathy is critical to this process, as people now interact regularly with strangers who come from different cultures and have different values.

Empathy is a skill that improves with practice. Canadian educator and social entrepreneur Mary Gordon has demonstrated that empathy can be effectively taught to elementary and middle school students. Her organization, Roots of Empathy, based in Toronto, helps tens of thousands of children acquire and apply this skill. The approach is novel: once a month, children receive a classroom visit from a baby and its parent, usually the mother, and an instructor who guides the lesson. The baby is deemed the "professor." During each visit, children are asked to observe and explain the baby's sounds, expressions, and movements, and to make connections with their own experiences. They learn to recognize and name the baby's feelings, which helps them to understand their own feelings and those of their classmates. Students in classes taught with Roots of Empathy engage in markedly less bullying and less social exclusion (the most stressful experiences for children) and learn to manage their emotions and peer interactions more successfully.

Democracies need citizens who can empathize and identify with others, recognize problems, and collaborate in building solutions. They need citizens who can stay focused on long-term objectives and face adversity without quitting. They need citizens who are prepared to take the lead in bringing change when necessary. Several years ago, for example, Ashoka reframed its vision from building the field of social entrepreneurship to building a world in which "everyone can be a changemaker." We believe these goals should be integrated into education beginning in grade school. Some may argue that it makes little sense to talk about educating children to be changemakers when we're having enough trouble teaching basic reading and math. But as innovative educators have shown, children become self-motivated to learn when their ideas are valued. Unfortunately, as Duckworth notes, if teachers are pressured to stay within narrow guidelines, they will have difficulty accepting the children's divergence and appreciating their creations.

Even math, a subject that currently drains the confidence of many, can be transformed into an enjoyable experience for all. John Mighton, founder of the Toronto-based organization Junior Undiscovered Math Prodigies (JUMP), has demonstrated in hundreds of classrooms that, contrary to conventional wisdom, the vast majority of students can learn to become comfortable with math. Mighton developed a curriculum and structure for managing classes that allows students of varying abilities to experience success at each stage of learning, no matter how they compare with their classmates. In *The Myth of Ability*, he argues that educators mistakenly prioritize cognitive over emotional aspects of learning. The first goal should be to build confidence because that leads to heightened attention and self-motivated effort. In classes taught with Mighton's methods, teachers report that children cheer when math period begins. It should come as no surprise that children enjoy progressively difficult challenges when there are opportunities to win at each level: that's the secret behind video games.

To encourage more people to be changemakers, schools should help students to believe (1) that their ideas are valuable; (2) that it is good to ask questions and take initiative; (3) that it is fun to collaborate with others; and (4) that it is far better to make mistakes than not to try at all.

In her book *Mindset: The New Psychology of Success*, psychologist Carol Dweck offers another way to reinforce such beliefs: provide feedback to children that draws attention to effort, rather than to intelligence or talent. Dweck has found that children who are praised for being "smart" actually become less persevering. They come to believe that their achievements stem from immutable natural abilities. Dweck calls this a "fixed" mindset, as opposed to a "growth" mindset, in which children are taught that their abilities and achievements are contingent on effort. She has observed that children with growth mindsets are more willing to admit mistakes and exhibit more determination in the face of adversity. These qualities are essential for social entrepreneurs.

The best way for schools to produce social entrepreneurs tomorrow is for them to encourage students to practice changemaking today. Youth-led social entrepreneurship is growing fast, but it operates largely outside the school system. Young people should study how other young people are successfully (or unsuccessfully) attacking social problems. Case studies taken from organizations like Youth Venture, Do Something, YouthNoise, Injaz, TakingITGlobal, Free the Children, the International Youth Foundation, or the Girl Scouts Challenge and Change program could easily be incorporated into class lessons. Currently, many schools promote service learning by engaging students in projects like cleaning up parks or distributing meals to the poor. These are worthy activities, but some students participate only because they are required to do so or because it looks good on a resume. A more innovative approach would be to expose students to serious problems and then challenge them to imagine and construct solutions, offering structured assistance to help them form organizations, raise funds, overcome bureaucratic hurdles, and evaluate their own work.

Finally, schools need to broaden the range of behaviors they encourage and reward. We celebrate academic achievement in the form of straight-A students who get into competitive high schools and top colleges; we celebrate athletes and gifted science students. (Winners of the Siemens Competition in Math, Science & Technology receive $100,000 prizes and national attention.) Schools should do more to celebrate youth-initiated social problem solving through award programs, conferences, and storytelling.

Students enlisted to think creatively about improving their school, community, or city will grow into more powerful citizens. For the rest of their lives, they will be oriented toward finding solutions to problems. Educators will discover, as numerous social entrepreneurs have already, that students so engaged become key allies—not just better learners, but cocreators of more effective and happier schools.

What is being done at the university level?

Over the past ten years, social entrepreneurship has made inroads into academia, but it remains far from mainstream. The first course in social entrepreneurship was initiated at Harvard University in 1994 by Greg Dees, who now leads the Center for the Advancement of Social Entrepreneurship at the Fuqua School of Business at Duke University. Today, approximately 350 professors in 35 countries teach such courses, according to the *Social Entrepreneurship Teaching Resources Handbook*, compiled by Debbi D. Brock of Berea College and Ashoka's Global Academy for Social Entrepreneurship.

Prominent schools, including Harvard University, New York University, and Oxford University, attract scholars interested in social entrepreneurship through competitive fellowship programs. Many leading business schools teach social enterprise and host social venture planning competitions. The Tata Institute of Social Sciences has developed the first MBA program in social entrepreneurship in India. In addition, social entrepreneurship has been integrated into curricula in schools of public policy, education, design, urban planning, public health, social work, law, engineering, environmental science, and technology. It has also been taken up in many community colleges. The primary impetus behind these changes has been student demand.

At present, social entrepreneurship does not have a standard curriculum. The University Network for Social Entrepreneurship, launched by Ashoka's Global Academy for Social Entrepreneurship and the Skoll Centre for Social Entrepreneurship at Oxford University, is building an online platform to assemble research and case studies from around the world. The question of where to situate and how to organize work that cuts across many academic disciplines has presented a practical challenge. Currently, the network places social entrepreneurship within the social sciences under the discipline of entrepreneurship. The *Stanford Social Innovation Review*, MIT's *Innovations* and the newly launched *Journal of Social Entrepreneurship*, edited by Alex Nicholls of Oxford University's Skoll Center, are, at present, the only journals in the field. Academics also publish in journals of management, entrepreneurship, organizational development, or public policy. To do so, they have to couch their ideas in the language of those disciplines.

Social entrepreneurship doesn't sit well within traditional disciplinary boundaries. Someone hoping to address a problem in health care, for example, may need supporting knowledge from other fields, such as history, administration, and finance. A would-be social entrepreneur would ideally be able to pursue studies in a variety of faculties, plus have the opportunity to earn credit through practical experimentation.

One structure that allows this is the Reynolds Program in Social Entrepreneurship at New York University, the first university-wide interdisciplinary fellowship program in the field. This pioneering initiative, housed in the Robert F. Wagner

Graduate School of Public Service, is open to undergraduate and graduate students from every school and discipline. It counts on high-level support from the university president to navigate the rough political waters of an academic institution. The Center for Public Leadership at Harvard's Kennedy School of Government also received support from the Catherine B. Reynolds Foundation to develop a fellowship program in social entrepreneurship. Harvard's program is more narrowly designed to shape entrepreneurial public service professionals. It remains open to students from the graduate schools of government, education, and public health.

Numerous universities, including Columbia, Stanford, the University of Michigan, University of Navarra, Spain, and the University of Geneva in Switzerland, have established partnerships with groups such as Ashoka, Echoing Green, New Profit, Inc., the Skoll Foundation, and the Schwab Foundation for Social Entrepreneurship. These partnerships bring students, faculty, and social entrepreneurs into regular contact. One of Ashoka's new initiatives with universities, Ashoka U, began by working with students, faculty, and staff members at Cornell, Johns Hopkins, George Mason, and the University of Maryland to help students recognize how they might advance change and strengthen social entrepreneurship teaching and research. Ashoka is now building a network of such campuses—spawning collaborative problem solving and integrating this kind of learning into the standard university education—so that schools reorient around the goal of fostering changemakers, rather than merely producing graduates.

These new university-practitioner partnerships are needed to generate research in many areas. Some pressing issues include finding better ways to assess impact, influence public policy, nurture entrepreneurial social leaders, finance and scale up organizations, and disseminate social innovations. The question of how to advance behavioral and attitudinal changes within large organizations and businesses—the practice of intrapreneurship—also needs more thorough examination.

Universities legitimize new fields and careers. They expose students to different pathways at critical junctures in their lives. They bring an independent view that can give a wider and longer perspective than practitioners in any one field. Universities are well positioned to serve as incubators for student- or faculty-led social innovation. They could establish social change laboratories to evaluate social experiments more rigorously, the way MIT has done with its Poverty Action Lab. (To attract more intrapreneurs, universities also need to offer alternatives to the publish-or-perish career path.)

The problem-solving patterns and insights emerging from the field of social entrepreneurship can be grasped only by stepping back. Universities need to take the lead in assembling this knowledge, classifying and analyzing it, and disseminating it so people can make use of the lessons. Only 2 percent of the world's population receives a college education. If important ideas are going to spread widely, those who enjoy access must share their knowledge with the other 98 percent. At a time when many scholars feel that academic research has grown detached from social priorities, the study of social entrepreneurship offers new opportunities for universities to address critical global needs.

While conducting research for his book *The Search for Social Entrepreneurship*, Paul Light surveyed 131 high-performing social organizations and found that their success depended less on the personality of their founders than on the disciplined application of (teachable) leadership and entrepreneurial skills. His research suggests that colleges and universities can, in fact, do a better job preparing students to think and behave like innovators. Groups like StartingBloc, the Transformative Action Institute and the newly created Unreasonable Institute address this need among select undergraduates and young professionals. Their models should be emulated and integrated more broadly into university programs.

To develop social entrepreneurs more systematically, universities could establish innovation funds to encourage student changemaking and stimulate collaborations with leading social organizations. They could use their surroundings as laboratories for social problem solving, just as land-grant universities employ "extension" workers to develop university research into practical applications that address the needs of farmers, engineers, families, and businesses in the university's home state. Universities can also offer courses in which students implement their ideas, receive guidance and feedback, and learn through practice much like medical residents learn from hands on training in hospitals.

Students should be invited to help shape curriculum, too. Today, many are insisting that courses in urban planning, business, design, and other disciplines address environmental and social concerns. Net Impact, an association of more than 10,000 socially concerned MBA students and graduates, advocates for such changes in business schools. Some universities have complied, but usually by adding elective courses in sustainable business or design rather than modifying core offerings in, say, finance or marketing (which usually omit sustainability considerations). These are typically added in response to student demand or due to the insistence of an internal champion. Universities could foster major changes by adopting the approach of schools like the Bainbridge Graduate Institute and the Presidio Graduate School, which integrate sustainability into every course.

One lesson of social entrepreneurship is that the character traits of leaders tend to be reflected in the institutions they build. Organizations that support social entrepreneurs look for high levels of integrity and trustworthiness in their candidates. Not only are such people more likely to build organizations that confer social benefits, but they are more likely to be successful in recruiting and retaining supporters. Recognizing this fact, universities with programs in social entrepreneurship often incorporate a social and emotional component that helps students reflect on their motivations, address fears and insecurities, and discover sources of resilience. They also build support by fostering a sense of community among students.

Universities are among the world's oldest enduring institutions. They change slowly, rarely voluntarily. Because they are so expensive to run, they like their alumni to succeed in lucrative fields so they can give generously to their alma mater. It will therefore require serious effort, primarily by students, to persuade them to prioritize the job of educating social change leaders.

What can governments do to engage more successfully with social entrepreneurs?

On all fronts—substance, politics, and staffing—social entrepreneurs have a great deal to offer governments. In almost every country where they are free to operate, social entrepreneurs can draw upon practical experiences to bring new ideas, problem-solving acumen, and organizational skill to improve government performance. They have demonstrated that it is possible to manufacture better outcomes in areas where governments have had difficulty achieving results.

Government leaders and social entrepreneurs face very different pressures and have distinct needs. Working together has thus often been a struggle. As mentioned, elected officials need to show results in a relatively short span of time in order to retain power. They are punished more for failure than they are rewarded for success. The big fear in government is not ineffectiveness, but scandals or failures that can be exploited by the opposition. Governments, therefore, face extreme demands for accountability. They often design policies around the methods of accountability. Governments also respect hierarchy and territory. They work by committee and strive for consensus.

Social entrepreneurs, in contrast, insist on being insulated from day-to-day political pressures. They take a long-term view to problem solving. They require flexibility, the freedom to pursue ideas that challenge vested interests, and the ability to experiment and fail. They work independently, and they disregard protocol and institutional boundaries when these prove to be obstacles.

Historically, the two sectors have suffered from a mutual lack of respect and trust. Social entrepreneurs have tended to regard policy makers and civil servants as "bureaucrats"— detached from the impact of their decisions; policy makers complain that social entrepreneurs fail to appreciate the complexities of running large systems. Many government officials make no distinction between social entrepreneurial organizations and run-of-the-mill nonprofits, while social entrepreneurs insufficiently appreciate creative efforts that emanate from public agencies.

These tensions have impeded necessary collaboration. In a poll taken at an international conference of social entrepreneurs in Brazil in 2005, 80 percent of attendees said they needed to work more closely with governments to increase their impact, but only 20 percent were actually working with their governments or had a plan to do so.

In the United States, a coalition of more than 80 social entrepreneurs called America Forward, under the leadership of New Profit Inc., working with the Center for American Progress, put forward a set of policy ideas that led the Obama administration to create a White House Office on Social Innovation and Civic Participation and to support an innovation fund, for which Congress appropriated $50 million in seed capital.

The new office works to identify and scale high-performing social organizations, forge partnerships with business and philanthropy, and support national service and other forms of citizen engagement. The fund is designed to leverage private investment to expand "ideas that work." The administration's recovery act also allocated $650 million for a "What Works Fund" within the Department of Education, to be invested in school and community initiatives with proven impact. Intrapreneurs within the administration hope to build upon these early steps to demonstrate how governments can improve their overall effectiveness by harnessing the power of social innovators outside government. In so doing, they hope to shape a policy environment more alert to the potential of social entrepreneurs and citizen organizations.

What many American policy makers do not yet appreciate is that social entrepreneurship is qualitatively different from the "thousand points of light" idea, which President George H. W. Bush invoked to celebrate small-scale, grassroots, community initiatives twenty years ago. Social entrepreneurship is no more a little helper to government than business entrepreneurship is a little helper to the U.S. Treasury. It is becoming a primary engine for the invention and deployment of solutions. Social entrepreneurship represents a fundamental reorganization of the problem-solving work of society: a shift from control-oriented, top-down policy implementation to responsive, decentralized institution building. It draws on a core insight of the twentieth century: namely, that a dynamic marketplace of ideas and initiative is the basis of a thriving economy. Under normal circumstances, governments understand this. When seeking to stimulate the economy, a government will look for ways to encourage enterprise; it won't start its own companies to satisfy consumer needs.

Ironically, this pattern is often reversed when it comes to education, health care, and other social functions. In the social sector, governments are actively engaged in running service enterprises, not just funding or overseeing them. These public structures were created to ensure equality and universal access, which continue to be vital considerations. However, governmental structures that are ill-suited to running businesses do not necessarily perform better when running organizations to address social needs. In many areas, organizations run by social entrepreneurs achieve superior results.

The solution is not to simply abolish ineffective government programs but for governments to change the way they deploy their resources. Rather than trying to create their own structures to address problems, governments should look to develop and harness the potential of social entrepreneurs and citizen organizations to achieve policy goals, just as they do with business entrepreneurs and companies. In the past, when governments identified promising innovations in the social sector, they would supplant the organizations and try to take the ideas to scale within government. This model, known as pilot and scale, made sense in theory. Some group would demonstrate an approach to a problem, say, an early childhood enrichment program; it would undergo a rigorous evaluation, and if the results were promising, the government would take up the idea and replicate it.

Most of the time, pilot and scale produced disappointing results for the simple reason that scaling an idea requires every bit as much entrepreneurship as piloting one. To scale an idea is to pilot the growth of that idea. Survival rates in business indicate that the growth phase is every bit as risky as the launch phase. Scaling requires continuous learning and adjustment, a job that takes more flexibility than governments, as currently structured, usually enjoy. We wouldn't think of asking a government agency to replicate a profitable business. What policy makers should recognize is that replicating a successful social organization is not that different.

To engage with social innovators more successfully, governments could systematically survey society for social entrepreneurs who have demonstrated results and growth potential and assist them in taking their ideas and organizations to scale. In doing so, the government should think like a gardener, rather than a builder. A gardener knows that he cannot make a plant grow. The best he can do is identify good seeds and soil, provide nourishment and protection from the elements, and keep a careful watch. Plants grow of their own volition. No one can mandate the healthy growth of an organism—and an organization attacking a tough social problem is very much like an organism. Its growth is a tenuous affair. Governments need new mechanisms to seed and grow social innovations. The Obama administration is now exploring this challenge with its What Works and Social Innovation funds.

To be successful, governments will have to shift from a model of running programs and purchasing services from low-cost providers to a model of investing in and providing different forms of assistance to high-performing institutions led by entrepreneurs. Some of these changes are underway in the field of international development in response to government's lackluster performance with aid projects and the superior achievements of social entrepreneurs. Historically, foreign aid was channeled almost exclusively through governments. Today, donors give more resources directly to citizen organizations. Microfinance played a major role accelerating this trend; social enterprise is poised to follow suit.

To make this shift, governments should focus on building respectful partnerships with outside groups that are implementing solutions. To help those organizations expand, they should shift from providing after-the-fact payments for services to front-loaded, equity-like investments that are large enough to fuel expansion plans and linked to performance. Governments need to find ways to oversee significant long-term investments in institutions, without assuming control of those institutions. And they will have to become skilled in communicating the rationale for this new approach to the press, because it will produce both successes and failures.

In addition, governments will need to overhaul the current framework of incentives and regulations that constrain social entrepreneurship, including social enterprise. Governments could do the following:

- Make it less burdensome for people to open and close social-purpose organizations
- Make it easier for citizens to receive tax benefits for contributions of money and in-kind services. (In many societies, citizens and corporations cannot claim tax deductions for charitable contributions.)

- Expand national service, leveraging AmeriCorps and Experience Corps-type programs to engage more citizens in problem solving
- Hold conferences of social entrepreneurs, policy makers, philanthropists, businesspeople, researchers, journalists, and others to identify new solutions, address blockages, and expand on success
- Create cross-sector fellowships to bring social entrepreneurs into government and place policy staffers in social organizations. Congressional staffers, legislative committees, and political campaign directors understand politics better than the particulars of solutions, while social entrepreneurs understand how to address problems but not the nuances of political deal making
- Introduce innovation funds within all government agencies for investment in high-performing institutions
- Engage with philanthropists and impact investors to encourage the development of a social capital market
- Modify the tax treatment of the newly created L3C (low-profit limited liability) corporation and other social-purpose businesses to make them more attractive to investors

Many of these ideas are already being explored at city, state, and national levels. In his study *Advancing Social Entrepreneurship: Recommendations for Policy Makers and Government Agencies*, Andrew Wolk describes numerous examples in which social entrepreneurs collaborate with governments to achieve policy goals. One example is ITNAmerica, a nonprofit transportation service for seniors that has received government assistance at all levels, including funding and policy support, to replicate its model in several cities. In Indianapolis, former mayor Bart Peterson and former Charter Schools Director David Harris created The Mind Trust to recruit education-focused social entrepreneurs to the city. Peterson's predecessor, Stephen Goldsmith, authored *Governing by Network: The New Shape of the Public Sector*, which also details how governments are forging new kinds of partnerships to tackle social problems more effectively than in the past.

It's important to emphasize that while governments are not necessarily the best actors to implement solutions, they remain responsible for the provision of solutions. Parents are responsible for their children's health care, even if they don't perform the vaccinations. Social entrepreneurship is not a replacement for government or a model for letting elected officials off the hook.

Governments and social entrepreneurs need one another. Because nobody elects social entrepreneurs, their legitimacy is subject to question. The government remains the only actor that represents the whole of society. Only governments have the capacity to address problems at national scale and provide equal access to all, regardless of ability to pay. A good example of the interplay between social entrepreneurship and government is the role played by Gifford Pinchot. A leading social entrepreneur in the American conservation movement and the first Chief Forester of the U.S. Forest Service, he fought in the early 1900s to advance a policy of federal ownership and management of public lands, an idea that led to the establishment of national forests and later national parks. Today, we can see the competitive weaknesses and advantages of government in our mail delivery. Federal Express may offer better service than the postal system, but the U.S. Postal Service provides the only way to send a letter across the country for less than 50 cents.

One of the principal effects of social entrepreneurship, as the field grows, will be to sharpen and refine the role of government. Social entrepreneurs will help to ease governments out of daily functions that they are not well-suited to perform—so they can focus on their competitive advantages: determining priorities, ensuring fairness, and fashioning a framework of incentives and oversights that can best unleash society's full creative potential in service to the public will. As James Madison wrote, the object of government is "the happiness of the people." But a good government must also understand "the means by which that object can be best attained."

How is social entrepreneurship influencing business?

The explosion of social entrepreneurship over the past quarter century occurred outside the purview of business. But today, leaders in both sectors are moving beyond the ideological blinders that have prevented them from recognizing opportunities to transform the way both sectors work to serve society. Social entrepreneurs appreciate the managerial and financial competence that distinguishes great companies, and, increasingly, business entrepreneurs are coming to respect the ingenuity and impact of effective social organizations.

In addition, businesspeople are recognizing that social entrepreneurship brings new opportunities to generate profits. Social entrepreneurs are proving to be the best access routes to large markets in both developing and industrialized countries that are currently underserved by traditional businesses. Just as innovation occurs at the intersection of fields—biology and computer science, for example—a great deal of innovation in the coming years will emerge at the intersection of the social and business sectors. Businesspeople stand to gain by understanding how social entrepreneurs identify opportunities, develop products, satisfy clients, motivate staff, handle distribution, and manage pricing in unfamiliar contexts.

Ignorance of the field of social entrepreneurship will also carry new risks for business. Firms increasingly maintain brand loyalty through their behavior as corporate citizens—including how they treat their employees and suppliers, how they protect the environment, and how their products contribute to society's well-being. Many talented employees avoid working for companies with lackluster social records, and some investors incorporate social concerns in their value determinations. Shareholder activists and social-rating agencies can now communicate with millions of stakeholders. Meanwhile, the regulatory environment is poised for change, with tougher social and environmental safeguards likely to come. These changes are occurring at the global level. Even in developing countries, companies that have long been indifferent to social concerns will not be able to count indefinitely on the passive acquiescence of millions of poor people.

These changes, along with an increase in the number of socially motivated entrepreneurs, may produce a synthesis between ordinary business and social enterprise, with the distinction between the two becoming less significant with time. The shifting demands of customers, employees, and investors may simply make it less practical, lucrative, and satisfying to operate businesses that focus only on profits. To be sure, many companies will continue to pursue harmful business practices. But innovative companies will recognize the new market signals and will adapt, just as they responded to technological changes over the past twenty-five years. Businesspeople familiar with the landscape of social entrepreneurship will be better prepared than their competitors to recognize and seize the opportunities.

In decades past, many people who were primarily motivated by social or ethical concerns did not view business as a pathway to realize their ambitions. Those who wanted to "make a difference" might have entered one of the caring professions—teaching, medicine, or the clergy, for example—or gone into journalism, science, or law. Or they may have pursued the bifurcated approach of John D. Rockefeller and Andrew Carnegie, who engaged in exploitative practices to make money and demonstrated public-mindedness when giving it away.

The global emergence of social enterprise challenges the idea that people go into business exclusively to make money. In *Creating a World without Poverty*, Muhammad Yunus contends that by reducing humans to "one dimensional" profit seekers, economic theory has produced a "narrow" interpretation of capitalism which has failed to "capture the essence of a human being." It has blinded people to other uses of business.

Today, many see social enterprise as a vehicle to satisfy a full spectrum of goals and desires. Social enterprise is taking off so quickly and in so many directions that it would require numerous books to give it adequate treatment. The need for this new approach is obvious. While markets are marvelous tools to coordinate economic activity, they regularly fail to meet many basic needs of the poor. For example, markets have not been able to deliver health insurance, effective education and day care, or even fresh fruits and vegetables to low-income people in the United States. It is social entrepreneurs who are today creating new kinds of marketplaces to make such things available at affordable prices. Similarly, entrepreneurs are developing systems to conscientiously extend credit and other financial services to the millions of "underbanked"

Americans who are routinely exploited by predatory lenders, used car dealerships, and check-cashing outlets. In another crucial area, "cleantech" firms are developing a wide array of products to reduce society's environmental footprint.

In the developing world, countless firms, both for-profit and nonprofit, are marketing to the four billion underserved people in the so-called "Bottom of the Pyramid," a term popularized by the business professor C. K. Prahalad in his influential book, *The Fortune at the Bottom of the Pyramid*. As microfinance has shown, poverty alleviation doesn't come from market access alone. Among the poor, the most pressing needs are not individual sachets of hair conditioner or skin cream but clean water, nutritious and affordable food, good housing, access to health care, education and information, and tools and transportation services that help them seize economic opportunities.

In recent years, social entrepreneurs have launched enterprises to provide many such necessities, including solar power, biomass fuels, and low-energy cooking stoves. They provide health products like reading glasses, hearing aids, and malaria nets. They offer sliding-scale cataract surgeries to villagers and sell low-cost prostheses to amputees. They run low-profit pharmaceutical firms to develop medicines for developing world illnesses that drug companies ignore. They serve the poor with income-generation tools such as foot-powered water pumps, turnkey bee-cultivation businesses, and soil-testing kits. They provide cell-phone-based banking, remittance, and farm data services. They help language translators, village-based artisans, and growers of coffee, tea, flowers, and cocoa gain access to new markets. They operate slum- or village-based Internet kiosks, distance learning programs, mobile laundromats, and ambulance services.

They help villagers launch microfranchise businesses. They sell microinsurance to protect the poor from illnesses, crop failures, and natural disasters.

Many of these enterprises are in early stages and are still experimenting to develop viable business models. Some, like Aravind Eye Care System in India, which has performed millions of surgeries, achieve profitability through cross-subsidization (sliding-scale pricing in which better-off customers pay more for the same services than poor people, who pay little or nothing). Collectively, they lack coordinated market supports, especially the financial services that traditional businesses count upon. As previously noted, building these supports will be the crucial next phase in the development of this field. The World Resource Institute's Web site, NextBillion.net, does an excellent job tracking developments in social enterprise. A new magazine, *Beyond Profit*, launched by Intellecap also chronicles the field.

Social entrepreneurs are also transforming business by forming partnerships with corporations to help them serve large numbers of poor people. Companies that hope to do business with the Bottom of the Pyramid, either as buyers or sellers, have the choice of spending years building new distribution channels and changing their corporate cultures or engaging in joint enterprises with social entrepreneurs who are already serving these markets.

Many companies have already begun this process. Yunus has formed a partnership with Danone Foods of France to create Grameen Danone, a new social business to market an inexpensive, fortified yogurt product to Bangladeshi villagers, particularly children. Grameen's goal is to address urgent health problems caused by micronutrient deficiencies. Danone gets to present itself as a good corporate citizen, offer employees an exciting project to work on, and gain exposure to a large new market.

Ashoka has created an initiative under its Full Economic Citizenship program that it calls the "Hybrid Value Chain," which helps businesses and social entrepreneurs conceive, organize, and finance partnerships to market products and services to underserved communities. For example, Ashoka has formed a partnership with the giant Mexican cement manufacturer Cemex, through which social entrepreneurs in its fellowship manage the sale of affordable building products on credit to slum dwellers. The company gains access to a new market, the social entrepreneurs gain an additional revenue source, and the clients get better housing.

In another example of this trend, Starbucks and Green Mountain Coffee Roasters have formed a partnership with Root Capital, a nonprofit social investment fund, to help source coffee from farming cooperatives in the developing world. In this case, Root Capital has provided capital for coffee-washing machines so farmers can meet the retailers' quality standards. By providing capital and training, and brokering market connections, the organization helps people in poor, environmentally vulnerable communities around the world achieve sustainable livelihoods.

The essence of these partnerships is complementarity. Businesses possess the capital and productive capacity to develop new products and market them at scale; social entrepreneurs understand the markets, have established distribution channels, and enjoy the customers' trust.

Businesses are also changing from within, led by intrapreneurs who are instituting processes to integrate social and environmental considerations into basic business management. Some of the most critical social and environmental changes in the coming years will originate in large corporations. For example, Kelly Lauber, who directs sustainable ventures at Nike, the global footwear and apparel company, spearheads an initiative called GreenXchange, which helps companies share intellectual property for green product design and manufacturing—things like water-based adhesives and "green rubber," which are far less toxic than traditional formulas. The biggest news on this front was Wal-Mart's announcement in July 2009 that it would be creating a "sustainability index" to assess the waste, water, and energy usage of every one of its 60,000 suppliers globally, a move that prompted excitement from even skeptical environmentalists.

These changes have been inspired by pathbreaking books like *The Ecology of Commerce* and *Natural Capitalism*, among others, and pioneering business leaders like Ray Anderson, whose global carpet manufacturing company, Interface, exemplifies sustainable business. R. Paul Herman, author of *The HIP Investor*, notes that such changes produce quantifiable social impact *and* "lead to higher revenues, lower costs, tax benefits, more enthusiastic and productive staff, and greater shareholder value."

Wal-Mart, like many businesses, began focusing on sustainability because of public pressure to account for things that it largely ignored in the past—pollution, resource depletion, workforce diversity, waste, sprawl, labor conditions in the developing world, and effects on families and communities. Wal-Mart has always focused on efficiency, and the company now anticipates considerable savings through its efforts to conserve energy and resources. Less innovative or dominant companies will likely enlist lobbyists and lawyers in an effort to maintain the status quo. It will take well-placed intrapreneurs at all levels of corporations to pioneer solutions, overcome resistance, and artfully advance change.

Social entrepreneurs are also changing the nature of corporate social responsibility, something treated in the past as little more than an extension of a company's public relations. For example, Philip Morris, the tobacco company, has long sought to dampen criticism by supporting museums and orchestras. Corporate grant-making foundations geared to marketing objectives have traditionally been more interested in good press than social impact.

Today, social responsibility is being recognized as a core management function, one that plays a key role in motivating and retaining employees, providing leadership opportunities, and strengthening relationships with customers. Social entrepreneurs, recognizing the value that they bring to companies, are increasingly eschewing corporate social responsibility departments in favor of dealing with top executives directly. They are pursuing front-door rather than side-door partnerships, and they are seeking more than financial assistance or sponsorships. Instead, they look to work with companies where there is a strategic alignment.

Companies that have developed robust, long-term partnerships with social entrepreneurs report benefits in their primary business activities. New Profit Inc. and Ashoka, for example, have helped the consulting firms Monitor and McKinsey respectively to recognize and serve new categories of clients. Through its partnerships with KaBOOM! and HandsOn Network, Home Depot provides opportunities for thousands of employees to engage in reliably enjoyable and meaningful service. And at a time when the book business is faring poorly, First Book has helped publishers recognize new market opportunities by reaching out to millions of low-income families who historically have been overlooked by booksellers.

Finally, social entrepreneurs are influencing the regulatory and investment environments to hold businesses more accountable to their social and environmental performance and to support social enterprise.

Oversight is crucial to ensure the integrity of social enterprise. Recently, a few cases have sparked debate about the potential for social enterprises to take advantage of poor customers, who often lack choice in the marketplace. The most controversial was the initial public offering by the microfinance lender Banco Compartamos in Mexico, which yielded staggering profits for its investors, including the nonprofit microfinance network ACCION International. At issue was the nearly 100 percent annualized interest rate that Compartamos charges to its low-income borrowers. Investors defended the practice as one necessary to attract capital to serve the millions still unbanked (many of whom borrow from loan sharks, at even higher rates). Critics consider these lending practices to be usury by another name, especially when they are sustained by an absence of competition. As some microfinance lenders and investors seek to emulate Compartamos' success, others are advancing a movement within microfinance to improve financial education among borrowers, evaluate social as well as financial performance, and toughen consumer protection standards.

While many advocates seek to impose new regulations on businesses, independent groups are developing transparent rating and branding systems to encourage (and pressure) companies to voluntarily comply with social and environmental performance standards. For example, Social Accountability International has developed the global standard SA8000, which certifies that companies maintain decent working environments.

B Lab has established the "B Corporation" certification, which companies receive only if they can demonstrate social benefits for *all* their stakeholders. HIP Investor has created scoring systems to help investors rank companies based on their combined human impact and profit. These and other new oversight tools, accessible to any investor or consumer, along with government regulatory changes and recognition of legal hybrids, such as the low profit limited liability corporation, will likely accelerate the growth of social enterprise in the coming decade.

Can philanthropy be more effective?

Philanthropy is potentially society's most innovative form of capital, but it is not always deployed effectively. Compared to policy makers and business investors, philanthropists can assume more risk, maintain a longer-term focus, and support less popular ideas. Philanthropists provided the seed funding for many of the most important social changes in the history of the United States. They financed abolitionists, suffragettes, labor organizers, citizens' rights groups, hospital builders, and universities and schools for the disabled—often long before the work was understood or publicly validated.

Philanthropy could dramatically increase the impact of the citizen sector in the coming decades. Researchers estimate that inheritances for the first half of the twenty-first century will amount to tens of trillions of dollars, a significant portion of which will be allocated for philanthropic purposes. The total annual expenditures of U.S. charitable organizations that currently report to the IRS is roughly $1 trillion.

In addition to the growth in resources, philanthropists are also experimenting with new models of financing that are better structured than past approaches to meet the needs of social innovators. For example, some provide loan guarantees and "first loss" funds to enable grantees to leverage capital markets; others use grants to catalyze innovation and seed new markets; still others make collaborative, multiyear "patient capital" investments to fuel the growth of proven organizations. These are some of the new approaches that have been described as "venture philanthropy," "strategic philanthropy," and "impact investing."

Historically, philanthropy was viewed through the lens of charity and often practiced in an unsystematic, even capricious, fashion. To be sure, many leading foundations, such as the Rockefeller, Ford, and Robert Wood Johnson foundations, have long maintained a sharp focus on results. But in years past, donors had a poor understanding about the effectiveness of their grants or the relative merits of giving opportunities. The standard approach was to provide modest-size, one-year grants restricted to specific uses, a method of financing which is poorly suited to the needs of institution builders.

Many foundations have also neglected to evaluate their own performance. In recent years, they have come under fire for this oversight. Critics argue that philanthropy, which confers tax benefits, should be accounted for like other public resources. In response to such criticisms and influenced by the rise of social entrepreneurship, many philanthropists have intensified their focus on measurable results. The most daring have even allowed themselves to be evaluated by their grantees, a trend which is to be encouraged.

Over the past decade, numerous donors, such as Venture Philanthropy Partners, New Profit Inc., Atlantic Philanthropies, the Robin Hood Foundation, and the NewSchools Venture Fund, have adopted an approach to giving that is modeled on venture capital financing. It involves multiyear grants that are usually combined with some kind of direct engagement on the part of the donors. This assistance may include management consulting, business plan development, research, networking, lobbying support, or assistance with marketing. Funding is often aggregated across donors and tied to a growth plan, rather than restricted to one program. One benefit of this approach is that grants will often be automatically renewed if organizations meet the performance targets specified in their plans. Though this may seem merely sensible, it represents a departure from the past, where grants were often renegotiated annually based on considerations that were far from transparent.

Groups like Bridgespan and Nonprofit Finance Fund Capital Partners help organizations develop growth strategies, while certain philanthropists target specific fields and institutional stages, developing expertise in those areas. For example, the Edna McConnell Clark Foundation and SeaChange Capital Partners provide growth funding only to organizations that aim to transform the lives of youths. Recently, the Skoll Foundation launched the Skoll Urgent Threats Fund, to support efforts to combat climate change, the Middle East conflict, nuclear proliferation, pandemics, and water scarcity.

All these factors are driving a shift from what might be termed "palliative" to "curative" philanthropy, in which donors seek less to mitigate suffering than to transform the social conditions that produce suffering. The major elements of this shift include searching for innovative ideas, targeting investment to high-performing social entrepreneurs, providing longer-term capital along with managerial assistance, and rigorously tracking results.

These changes have been widely adopted by the current generation of high-tech entrepreneurs-cum-philanthropists—many of whom made fortunes while still in their 30s and 40s and will be active well into the twenty-first century. In contrast to more traditional philanthropists, they have demonstrated a desire not simply to write checks but to get directly involved in the construction of solutions.

Joel L. Fleishman, in his book *The Foundation: A Great American Secret*, predicts that social entrepreneurship and venture philanthropy will come to dominate philanthropy in the twenty-first century because these models for organizing and financing social change "significantly overachieve in impact the dollars spent the old-fashioned way." However, one significant limitation of venture philanthropy is that, unlike start-up businesses, social organizations don't generate profits when they are successful. Nor do they typically enjoy economies of scale. There is no exit strategy; as they grow, they just need more money. The venture capital approach is designed to support enterprises in their early stages, not in perpetuity. For ongoing needs or major growth funding, social entrepreneurs must look to governments or large donor pools, or generate their own revenues through social enterprise. The latter is attracting growing interest among philanthropists. A number have created so-called patient capital funds to fulfill the institution-building function that private equity funds serve for business.

The landscape of giving is also broadening in other ways. Organizations such as GlobalGiving and Kiva are harnessing the Internet to aggregate resources from millions of individual "micro" philanthropists. Other examples of resource aggregators include giving circles, women's foundations, and town associations. The old model of strangers giving to strangers is being replaced by one based on connection and accountability.

Below are some ideas about how philanthropists might redeploy resources to harness social entrepreneurs more effectively:

Help social entrepreneurs engage more successfully with businesses and governments

The world's largest foundation—the Bill and Melinda Gates Foundation—gave away $3.5 billion in 2009. That might sound like a huge sum, but it is less than the annual budget of the New York City Police Department. The Gates Foundation hopes to make a dent in global poverty and health with its money. Therefore, the foundation needs leverage. One approach is to support social entrepreneurs who have the potential to shift practices in business and government. First, policy makers and social entrepreneurs need to be brought together more regularly so they can find ways to combine their strengths to improve public systems. And social entrepreneurs and business leaders need to form partnerships so they can discover how to transform business practices to meet pressing needs. The process of convening these parties, sharing ideas, and building trust is time-consuming and costly. Philanthropists are uniquely positioned to catalyze such exchanges and to create the neutral space conducive for incubating new ideas and institutions.

Fund structural supports for social entrepreneurship

Philanthropists could use their influence with universities to encourage education and research focused on social entrepreneurship. They could provide tuition support to attract students who are interested in this field. Existing fellowship programs, like those run by Echoing Green, the Draper Richards Foundation, Ashoka, or The Mind Trust, play a key role nurturing talent for the field of social entrepreneurship. But they are highly limited in number. Many fellowship programs are needed to attract more people into the field and, in particular, to recruit entrants from low-income families, who often assume considerable financial risk when they depart from conventional career paths.

Social entrepreneurship remains underreported. Foundations could address this problem by investing in new media structures that incorporate more coverage of solutions in the news. They could also support the creation of platforms (journals, Web sites, public databases, etc.) to facilitate knowledge sharing about social innovation. The Skoll Foundation's Web site, Social Edge, provides a space for social entrepreneurs to write about their experiences, exchange advice, and learn about events and opportunities, such as fellowship and funding programs. Ashoka's Changemaker Web site hosts "collaborative competitions," in which people around the world propose solutions to global problems. This open-source format pulls in many practical ideas, the best of which are rewarded with prizes and sometimes large foundation grants. Foundations with research staffs should also do more to help small grant makers identify strategic giving opportunities.

Foundations could fund training programs and fellowships to help baby boomers make the transition to changemaking in their "encore careers," a strategy that Marc Freedman, author of *Encore*, deems necessary for society to realize a vast "experience dividend" from the "biggest generation in American history." Foundations could also support programs that provide "service grants" to companies, following the model of the Taproot Foundation, so as to integrate pro bono work more closely with business careers and ensure that firms remain socially engaged during recessions. These exposures increase the flow of talent across sectors. Finally, philanthropists could leverage their existing investments by supporting the growth of more advisory services, like FSG Social Impact Advisors, which help philanthropists and social investors make smarter funding decisions.

Stick with things that work and communicate clearly

In business, investors change strategies when they believe they can get better returns. Philanthropists, policy makers, and political appointees frequently change directions when they seek variety or simply hope to distinguish themselves from their predecessors. One example is UNICEF's shift away from child survival. Between 1982 and 1995, UNICEF helped orchestrate astonishing gains in children's health by drawing global attention to a few basic life-saving interventions. Millions of deaths were prevented, largely through vaccinations and oral rehydration therapy. When UNICEF's leadership changed in 1995, the push for child survival fell off—not because results were poor or the need was gone—but because the new leader had a preference for rights-based interventions.

Similarly, funders often change tacks for reasons concealed from their grantees, terminating relationships with explanations like, "We've been working together for several years and we feel it's time to move on." This is closer to the language of courtship than social investing. When funders communicate this way, they send the message that performance is secondary. Funders should make efforts to explain their decisions along the following lines: "We believe we can have more impact elsewhere—and here's why."

Let more organizations die

Every day, new social organizations open their doors, but few close down or merge. Because the social arena lacks the institutional turnover that one finds in the business sector, resources tend to be spread ever more thinly over time, rather than reallocated from low- to high-performing groups. Industries need a continual replenishment of ideas, people, and organizations or they stagnate. The solution is not to discourage people from starting ventures, but merely to ensure that failure and mediocrity lead to reductions or withdrawal of funding.

Help social entrepreneurs work together

Bill Drayton contends that the next major stage for social entrepreneurship is to improve collaboration. Early in the twentieth century, groups of lawyers and management consultants discovered that they could gain efficiencies and multiply their influence by joining together in firms. Philanthropy could encourage social entrepreneurs to join together in firms, as well, where they could share expertise and contacts, test ideas, launch ventures, and provide consulting services to larger clients, including businesses and governments. Such firms could furnish a home base to reduce the risk and loneliness that can discourage early-stage entrepreneurs. Successful initiatives along these lines include the Centre for Social Innovation and the MaRS Discovery District, both in Toronto. Another creative collaboration is Social Innovation Generation, a partnership between the J.W. McConnell Family Foundation, the MaRS Discovery District, the PLAN Institute, and the University of Waterloo, which works to foster economic, cultural and policy changes in Canada that are conducive to continuous social innovation and "whole system" reforms.

How will the field of social entrepreneurship influence journalism?

Journalism is undergoing a profound transformation as traditional media sources, particularly newspapers and network news shows, experience drops in readers and viewers. During

2009, more than one hundred American newspapers closed or stopped publishing a print edition. Even the survival of a printed version of the mighty *New York Times* remains in question. As consumers continue to migrate to online and cable media, it is unclear what tomorrow's news sources will look like and how they will be financed.

One change that social entrepreneurship may advance is the legitimizing of a category of news focused on solutions. Mainstream news today is dominated by information about problems and stories of conflict. Most of the activity in the field of social entrepreneurship remains hidden from public view. Consider the Grameen Bank, arguably the world's most celebrated anti-poverty organization. In three decades, the *New York Times* has referred to the bank in 84 stories, a third of them since Grameen won the Nobel Peace Prize in 2006. By contrast, it referred to the Tamil Tigers in eight hundred stories and the Irish Republican Army in 3,600. The phrases "drug gangs" and "drive by shooting" each bring up close to six hundred stories. Since 1981, the *Times* has mentioned Ashoka in sixteen articles, BRAC in seven, the Self-employed Women's Association in eight, and ShoreBank in twenty-eight. These organizations, all considered among the world's preeminent examples of social entrepreneurship, have each been operating for thirty years. Each boasts a wealth of experience in attacking poverty and other problems—experience that, if better understood, could improve public policy and help thousands of social organizations achieve superior results. But news editors who are comfortable covering a large company like IBM or a sports team like the Yankees on a regular basis believe that they should not report on an important social organization more than once or twice in a year.

Solution stories, when they appear, tend to be treated as secondary or "soft" news compared to reports of corruption in business or government, for example. There is nothing in the nature of journalism that requires news to be overwhelmingly negative. News can be thought of as destabilizing information—information that shows how tomorrow will be different—and social entrepreneurship certainly upsets the status quo. The main role of a free press is to provide citizens with the information they need to lead good lives and to help society improve. Citizens need to be apprised of opportunities as well as problems.

Because of cultural biases and structural constraints within news organizations, however, journalists systematically underreport solutions. Journalists fear being labeled advocates. It's professionally safer to critique yesterday's events than to show appreciation for an idea that may hold promise for tomorrow. Newsroom budget cuts have also made it difficult for journalists to cover solutions, which often require more in-depth reporting than typical news stories. And it goes without saying that negative news, especially scandals and murders, sell newspapers. As a result, we know a great deal about what is broken in society but little about what is being done to fix things. The challenge today is to cover the field of social entrepreneurship faithfully. The media has a vital role to play making society's social problem-solving activity visible, illustrating, as we do in business every day, what leading entrepreneurs are doing and how industries are evolving.

This situation is poised for change. In polls, news consumers consistently indicate their dissatisfaction with the state of journalism. Journalists are also unhappy. Too often market imperatives in media companies override a concern for the public interest. Many reporters who entered the field with high hopes of improving society now struggle to remain true to their own ethical standards. Frustrated journalists will either force changes from within or build new media organizations.

Much has been made of the destabilizing effects of online media. Less has been said about how news companies are failing to adapt to the changing tastes of a generation of consumers who wish to be informed about problems *and* solutions. Forward-thinking universities and colleges have responded to student demand for change. Smart companies retain young employees by offering meaningful work and service opportunities. News companies need to recognize that journalists and consumers alike are eager for changes in the structure and content of the news that will help them reconnect to meaningful pursuits.

Social entrepreneurship offers a landscape of compelling stories. These are not just feel-good stories to lighten things up or provide a little seasonal fare at holiday time but vital information about how citizens are wielding power to reshape society. They are stories about new ideas, new career paths, and new institutions.

We have already seen the beginnings of change, as mainstream news sources have begun devoting marginally more attention to social entrepreneurs, albeit in the old-style good-news format often pegged to Thanksgiving or Christmas. Some examples are *CNN Heroes*, the *Frontline/World Social Entrepreneurs* series, intermittent profiles on ABC and NBC News, *20/20*, and *60 Minutes*, and features on social entrepreneurship in *Fast Company, Business Week*, and The *Economist*, as well as the reporting of journalists such as Matthew Bishop, Cheryl Dahle, Atul Gawande, Tracy Kidder, Nicholas D. Kristof, Jay Mathews, Tina Rosenberg, and Paul Tough, who have chronicled the work of social innovators in a variety of fields. Several targeted magazines also cover social innovation, including *Good* magazine, *Ode, Yes!*, and *Beyond Profit*, as well as online sites, including Social Innovation Conversations, GRITtv, Huffington Post Impact, and change.org, where Nathaniel Whittemore writes an excellent blog on social entrepreneurship.

Journalism will play a critical role in helping society to become more innovative. Social entrepreneurs depend on a responsive media to spread new ideas and challenge existing attitudes and behaviors. As more people get involved in the construction of solutions, they will require information that helps them to be effective. The news industry will, therefore, require comparatively more journalists who are both good storytellers and familiar with the mechanics of social problem solving. We will need journalists who can tell whether a social organization is outperforming or underperforming the "market." Discernment will be critical. Today's journalists know which companies in a given industry are most competitive and which politicians are accumulating power, but few can say which social organizations are transforming people's lives and which ones are just wasting money. Journalists will have to expand their core role from exposing problems to exposing both problems and opportunities.

A number of social entrepreneurs have begun to transform journalism by creating new platforms to produce and assemble news and foster greater public accountability. Many are working in developing countries where the media has historically been weak. Examples include La Silla Vacía (the Empty Seat), a news Web site that reveals the workings of political power in Colombia, and Groundviews, which provides a safe space for citizen journalism under conditions of severe censorship in Sri Lanka. Some aggregate voices from disparate sources. Global Voices Online integrates news coverage from around the world in a multilingual, searchable format, and New American Media helps thousands of small ethnic news organizations in the United States—the fastest growing sector of American journalism—reach wider audiences.

Other social entrepreneurs are building new systems to evaluate journalism and provide government oversight. Two examples are NewsTrust, a community-based service that rates articles based on credibility and quality, not just popularity, and Parliament Watch, a site in Germany that connects citizens directly with parliamentarians, fostering surprising levels of transparency. Several of these initiatives have received support from Ashoka's News and Knowledge program, which was initially funded by the John S. and James L. Knight Foundation and is designed to advance social entrepreneurship in the field of journalism.

As more journalists provide in-depth coverage of social entrepreneurship, it may improve news coverage in other areas. One lesson social entrepreneurs can teach journalists is that failure is necessary for innovation. Making mistakes and learning from them is the only guaranteed way to produce better ideas. Science and business journalists understand this, but those who cover public entities make little allowance for failure. Nor do they distinguish between excusable failures (i.e., mistakes that are part of the normal problem-solving process) and failures that are due to negligence or incompetence. If social or business entrepreneurs were covered like public officials, they would be far less bold and action-oriented. By covering social entrepreneurship more thoroughly, journalists may come to recognize the importance of providing tough oversight that does not unduly inhibit public sector experimentation.

*How can individuals prepare themselves to participate
in the field of social entrepreneurship?*

In his book *Blessed Unrest,* Paul Hawken traces the outlines
of a growing global movement that is comprised of *millions*
of mostly new organizations devoted to ecological sustainability and social justice. Trying to appreciate the "breadth of
the movement," he explains, "is like trying to hold the ocean
in your hand." Because the movement is diverse and decentralized, and activism is not its primary form of action, it has
attracted less attention than movements of the past. Nevertheless, Hawken argues that it carries the possibility for genuine
transformation. In a 2009 commencement address to students,
he said: "[T]he earth needs a new operating system. You are
the programmers, and we need it within a few decades."

Oliver Wendell Holmes wrote that a person "should share
the passion and action of his time at peril of being judged not
to have lived." A few months after entering office, President
Obama made the following appeal to the nation: "We need your
service right now, at this moment in history. I'm asking you to
stand up and play your part. I'm asking you to help change
history's course, put your shoulder up against the wheel." As
ordinary people step up in greater numbers to advance change
against tough odds—in campuses and companies, suburbs and
slums, farms and factories, deserts and jungles, schoolrooms and
skyscrapers—we need to investigate how each of us can best
prepare to participate in the "passion and action" of *our* time.

Peter Drucker, in his book *Management Challenges for the 21st
Century,* argued that in the coming years, individuals will not
be able to rely on institutions to guide their careers and lives.
The traditional boundaries between professions, industries,
and sectors will become blurred. We will have to navigate in
a shifting landscape. For compass points, each person should

seek to understand how his or her values and strengths inter-
sect with the changing needs of society. This is where we can
make our greatest contribution.

Understanding how to engage successfully with the field of
social entrepreneurship begins with self-knowledge. Students
frequently inquire about how to decide where to apply their
energies. They want to know whether to become a social entrepreneur or join an organization, or whether to focus on, say,
environmental issues or poverty. Finding the answers to such
questions hinges on personal considerations that each person
needs to explore for him or herself: What do you care deeply
about? What environments bring out your natural gifts? Are
you comfortable with uncertainty? Do you have a strong need
for autonomy?

Whatever your temperament, given the many roles opening
up in the field, there is no need to force yourself into a shape
that feels wrong. Most people who want to make a difference
are not organization founders. Fewer than one in ten American workers are self-employed. Most people prefer to work
in established structures, though that doesn't mean they have
to accept those structures as they are. Many advance change
within businesses and public institutions.

For everyone who starts an enterprise, hundreds are needed
to manage organizations, advocate for them, handle the technology, the finances, the communications, the training, and so
forth. It's like the movie business. Producers and directors are
not enough to make films. Actors, editors, technicians, ticket
vendors, reviewers, and audience members are all essential
to the enterprise. In the coming years, researchers, investors, policy makers, managers and storytellers, among many
others, will participate in the remaking of the field of social
entrepreneurship.

The importance of self-knowledge goes beyond understanding your strengths or leadership style, as important as these may be. A person who cares enough to commit wholeheartedly to an idea is usually acting on an interest whose seeds were planted years before, perhaps as far back as childhood. The first step for anyone embarking on a career in the field of social entrepreneurship is to determine what you have *always* cared about. In the archaeology of your life—past actions, relationships, studies, and work—unearth the artifacts of your abiding interests or your calling. The more honest your intention, the more genuine your attachment to the work, the more effective you will be—and the more fulfilled. This is critical because many social entrepreneurs struggle for years in obscurity before they achieve success and recognition.

In *The Courage to Teach*, Parker Palmer shows how one's inner life manifests itself inexorably in the outer world. Because changemakers seek to impose their *will* on society, they need to understand their motivations, if only to avoid doing unintended harm. Many social entrepreneurs recognize this responsibility and seek counsel from pastors, therapists, life coaches, mentors, and consultants. Some take personality tests to learn how to interact more successfully with others. Even as they lead institutions, many struggle with their own self-doubts and anxieties, powerful emotions that, if left unexamined, can damage relationships and undermine impact. As Palmer notes, if we want our social structures and businesses to reflect enlightened human values, we need leaders who are willing to engage in self-examination.

For those who choose to initiate social change organizations, the first practical challenges will be figuring out how to support yourselves while launching your organization. Some people keep a paid job and develop their ideas in their spare time. A small number receive stipends from organizations like Echoing Green, the Draper Richards Foundation, and other funders that provide early stage support. Some move in with friends or family to cut their personal expenses temporarily. Some ask their spouses or partners to be the primary or sole breadwinner for a period. Professionals, such as doctors or lawyers, may continue in their practices on a part-time basis to supplement the income they receive from their organizations. Many turn to family and friends for initial donations or investments.

Building an organization is a process of cultivating relationships. It is about calling people up and saying, "May I come talk with you?" Social entrepreneurs regularly draw in classmates, teachers, and former colleagues. As a rule, they don't recruit based on friendship alone. They look to work with people with similar values, especially those who can compensate for their own weaknesses.

Do a "market" survey. If you are concerned with addressing environmental problems, for example, it's a good idea to narrow your focus to one area—political action around global warming, for example, or something as specific as methods for reducing agricultural water waste. Then list the five most important innovations occurring in that field. You may have to look at fifty examples to come up with five ideas. It may take months of conversations and reading, but by the end of the process you should be familiar with the range of problems, approaches, and actors in that field. You will then be in a position to spot patterns and identify gaps. As you develop your idea, write down your plans. Even a two-page concept paper can lend an idea a tangible quality that generates its own momentum. The plan becomes a basis for discussion. Massive changes begin with asking someone what they think of your plan.

People get involved with ideas because they are excited by the opportunity to build something they care about. Always find out how your idea fits into another person's visions for his or her life. If someone asks, "How can I help you?" be ready with a few ideas—not just a request for money—but advice, references, introductions, moral support.

Open-mindedness is a prerequisite for innovation, but only to a point. Creating anything new involves an extraordinary amount of listening. On the other hand, to take the initiative we must believe that we know enough to get started. It requires a balancing act to remain open to what the world has to teach you, without losing sight of what you have to teach the world. How do you distinguish between advice to heed and advice you can safely ignore? Think of this question as an opportunity to clarify your motivation. When you peel back the layers of an idea, what remains at the core must be bedrock: an insight or belief that *grips* you with its power—something you *know* to be 100 percent true. The degree to which you operate from an unshakable core is the degree to which you can navigate the winding road, sort out the signal from the noise, and withstand criticism, opposition and failure.

To become a successful changemaker, you don't have to study social entrepreneurship. You do need to understand the workings of the systems you hope to change and the history of the problem with which you are concerned. Knowing how people have attempted to solve this problem in the past— what worked, what failed, and why—is essential because most new ideas are adaptations of earlier ideas that became bogged down by the details. Understanding those details may be the difference between achieving impact or failure. In addition to empathy, patience, and courage, you need hard skills: knowledge integral to building organizations—like finance, distribution, or marketing. "Today's world needs more than humanitarians," explains Jacqueline Novogratz in *The Blue Sweater*. "We need individuals who know how to listen and who have real and tangible skills to share. We will succeed only if we fuse a very hard headed analysis with an equally soft heart."

One group of changemakers who will play increasingly important roles will be those with cross-sectoral and cross-cultural experiences and relationships. Bridges between government, business, and the citizen sector, and across industries and borders, are necessary for the creation of whole solutions. Intermediaries will lead this process.

Above all, changemakers should learn how to navigate through resistance. Change always brings resistance. It is rarely rational. In *Leading Change*, James O'Toole explains that people resist change primarily because they bristle at the idea of having the will of others imposed upon them. They then concoct moral justifications to defend their positions. As psychologist Jonathan Haidt has noted, the mind looks for ways to make sense of what the gut has already decided.

For this reason, moral arguments alone rarely change minds. Being effective often means letting others believe they are right. People will endure the discomfort of self-questioning only if they feel appreciated and secure. Successful change-makers lower defenses in opponents by listening, acknowledging their ideas, and showing deference. Senator Edward Kennedy became one of the most effective legislators in U.S. history by developing collegial relationships with Republican lawmakers who virulently disagreed with him about the role of government. In similar fashion, social entrepreneurs like Geoffrey Canada of the Harlem Children's Zone, Vanessa Kirsch of New Profit Inc., and Wendy Kopp of Teach For

America have enlisted support from leaders across the U.S. political spectrum.

Of course, social change often needs to be *imposed*. The nation had to enact civil rights legislation in the 1950s and 1960s. But over the long run, the deepest changes in behavior and attitude are rooted not in laws but in feelings. Any change strategy that, in practice, causes undue humiliation or resentment will inevitably undercut itself. Look at the backlash against "political correctness," an example of a good idea— respect for otherness—too often advanced tactlessly. By contrast, a deceptively small step—draining the anger from an argument—turning a confrontation into an exchange—can create an opening for a shift in perspective.

As the citizen sector continues to mature, pathways currently unseen will emerge. Just as those who were free to relocate to Silicon Valley in the early 1990s could take maximum advantage of the Internet boom, those who remain mobile today—untethered to expensive life-styles—will be able to seize opportunities in social entrepreneurship as they arise. If the idea of active citizenship resonates with you, the place to begin is wherever you happen to be at the moment. We don't have to postpone action until we graduate or retire. We learn how to cause change by practicing changemaking now. We can bring change in our workplaces, schools, neighborhoods, or families, and in our selves. One simple way to strengthen commitment is to investigate a problem that deepens your understanding and draws you into caring and respectful relationships with people whom you can help.

If there is one overarching aspect of social entrepreneurship that remains misunderstood, it is the notion that you must be selfless to do this work. Journalists often refer to social entrepreneurs as do-gooders, conjuring up images of self-sacrifice.

The irony is that most social entrepreneurs we know find their work fulfilling and enjoyable. In contrast, polls reveal that the majority of doctors, lawyers, and journalists, for example, are dissatisfied with their work. People who switch to the field of social entrepreneurship after spending years doing more "sensible" work often say that they did so in order to feel more alive. Ask Jordan Kassalow, the founder of VisionSpring, which makes eyeglasses available to poor people in the developing world. He feels a thrill every time he sees a client's face light up with the experience of clear sight. His motivation for building VisionSpring into an international organization is crystal clear: "I get to experience that thrill over and over."

THOUGHTS FOR CHANGEMAKERS

1. Begin with an end in mind.
2. Do what you do best.
3. Have people ask you questions about your idea.
4. Practice pitching your idea.
5. Study the history of the problem you are attacking.
6. Develop a theory of change.
7. Keep thinking about how you can measure or evaluate success.
8. Celebrate every victory, no matter how small.
9. Initiate new relationships.
10. Apprentice yourself with masters. (Work without pay if necessary.)
11. Volunteer for a political campaign.
12. Publish a letter to the editor or an op-ed.
13. Meet with a newspaper editor and a congressman.
14. Host dinner discussions about your idea.
15. Form a group to achieve a modest, short-term goal.
16. Ask a question at a public forum.
17. Engage people with opposing political views.
18. Ask for advice from people you admire.
19. Read biographies of people who have built things.

20. Spend some time working in a different sector, field or country.
21. Practice public speaking.
22. Take a finance course.
23. Learn how to negotiate.
24. Find sources of inspiration and use them.
25. Hold to principles, be flexible about methods.

Trends in shifting mindsets

From	To
Expecting others to solve problems	Up to me/us
Big problems are too complicated to fix	We can solve problems at scale
Planned division of labor	Integrated, decentralized, emergent
Deficit based	Strengths based
Bureaucratic/hierarchical	Flexible teams of teams
Linear, top-down	All-direction, viral
Quarterly returns	7th-generation equity
Great men theories of change	Everyone can be a changemaker
Search for a cause	Make change from where you stand
Disposability	Cradle to cradle
Top-down design	Cocreation
Sustainability	Continuous renewal

A short list of online resources

1. Alltop's Social Entrepreneurship coverage (http://social-entrepreneurship.alltop.com)
2. Catalyst Fund's Social Business Blog (http://www. clearlyso.com/sbblog)
3. Change.org's Social Entrepreneurship blog, by Nathaniel Whittemore (http://socialentrepreneurship.change.org)
4. CSR Wire, a wire service for corporate social responsibility (http://www.csrwire.com)
5. Dowser, a media site that focuses on uncovering stories of change, founded by David Bornstein (www.dowser.org)
6. E-180's Top 25 social entrepreneurship websites (http://e-180.com/2009/02/04/our-top-25-social-entrepreneurship-websites)
7. Echoing Green's top social entrepreneurship blogs (http://www.echoinggreen.org/blog/top-seven-social-entrepreneurship-blogs)
8. Evan Carmichael's top 50 social entrepreneurship blogs 2009 (http://evancarmichael.com/Tools/Top-50-Social-Entrepreneur-Blogs-To-Watch-In-2009.htm)
9. Fast Company's "Ethnomics" (http://www.fastcompany. com/topics/ethonomics)
10. Global Voices Online, a leading participatory media news site focusing on the developing world (http://globalvoicesonline.org)
11. Good Magazine (http://www.good.is)
12. Greenbiz, coverage of green business (http://greenbiz. com)
13. Grist, green issues and sustainable living (http://www. grist.org)

14. MIT Innovations (http://www.mitpressjournals.org/
    loi/itgg)
15. Net Impact, global network of young business leaders
    seeking social impact (http://www.netimpact.org)
16. NextBillion.net, an initiative of the World Resources
    Institute, provides an overview of social enterprise
    globally (http://www.nextbillion.net)
17. Ode Magazine (http://www.odemagazine.com)
18. Social Edge, an initiative of the Skoll Foundation, is an
    online community for social entrepreneurs and other
    practitioners (http://www.socialedge.org)
19. Social Enterprise Alliance (http://www.se-alliance.org/
    index.cfm)
20. Stanford Social Innovation Review (http://www.
    ssireview.org)
21. Starting Bloc, educates and connects emerging leaders
    to drive social innovation (http://www.startingbloc.
    org/home)
22. Treehugger green news, solutions and product
    information (http://www.treehugger.com)
23. University Network for Social Entrepreneurship
    (http://universitynetwork.org)
24. World Changing, a media site focusing on major social
    issues (http://www.worldchanging.com)
25. Youth Social Entrepreneurs of Canada (http://www.ysec.
    org)

SELECTED BIBLIOGRAPHY

Books and articles referenced in the text

Bakan, Joel. *The Corporation: The Pathological Pursuit of Profit and Power*. New York: Free Press, 2004.

Baumol, William J. *The Free-Market Innovation Machine: Analyzing the Growth Miracle of Capitalism*. Princeton, N.J.: Princeton University Press, 2004.

Bishop, Matthew, and Michael Green. *Philanthrocapitalism: How the Rich Can Save the World*. New York: Bloomsbury Press, 2008.

Brock, Debbi. D., and Ashoka's Global Academy for Social Entrepreneurship. *Social Entrepreneurship Teaching Resources Handbook: For Faculty Engaged in Teaching and Research in Social Entrepreneurship*. Arlington, Virginia: Ashoka, 2008 (http://www.universitynetwork. org/handbook).

Collier, Paul. *The Bottom Billion: Why the Poorest Countries Are Failing and What Can Be Done About It*. New York: Oxford University Press, 2007.

Crutchfield, Leslie, and Heather McLeod Grant. *Forces for Good. The Six Practices of High-Impact Nonprofits*. San Francisco: Jossey-Bass, 2007.

Dorsey, Cheryl and Lara Galinsky. *Be Bold: Create a Career with Impact*. New York: Echoing Green, 2006.

Drucker, Peter. *Management Challenges for the 21st Century*. New York: Harper Business, 1999.

Duckworth, Eleanor. *The Having of Wonderful Ideas: And Other Essays on Teaching and Learning*. New York: Teachers College Press, 2006.

Dweck, Carol. *Mindset: The New Psychology of Success*. New York: Ballantine Books, 2007.

Elkington, John and Pamela Hartigan. *The Power of Unreasonable People: How Social Entrepreneurs Create Markets That Change the World*. Cambridge, Mass.: Harvard Business School Press, 2008.

Fleishman, Joel. *The Foundation: A Great American Secret*. New York: Public Affairs, 2007.

Florida, Richard. *The Rise of the Creative Class: And How It's Transforming Work, Leisure, Community and Everyday Life*. New York: Basic Books, 2002.

Freedman, Marc. *Encore: Finding Work That Matters in the Second Half of Life*. New York: Public Affairs, 2007.

Freireich, Jessica, and Katherine Fulton, *Investing for Social and Environmental Impact*, Monitor Institute 2009 (http://www.monitorinstitute.com/impactinvesting).

Gardner, John. *Self-Renewal: The Individual and the Innovative Society*. New York: Norton, 1995.

Goldsmith, Steven, and William D. Eggers. *Governing by Network: The New Shape of the Public Sector*. Washington D.C.: Brookings Institution Press, 2004.

Gopnik, Alison, Andrew N. Meltzoff, and Patricia K. Kuhl. *The Scientist in the Crib: What Early Learning Tells Us About the Mind*. New York: Harper Paperbacks, 2000.

Hawken, Paul, Amory Lovins, and L. Hunter Lovins. *Natural Capitalism: Creating the Next Industrial Revolution*. New York: Little, Brown, 1999.

Hawken, Paul. *Blessed Unrest: How the Largest Movement in the World Came into Being and Why No One Saw it Coming*. New York: Viking, 2007.

Hawken, Paul. *The Ecology of Commerce: A Declaration of Sustainability*. New York: HarperCollins, 1993.

Heilbroner, Robert. *The Worldly Philosophers: The Lives, Times and Ideas of the Great Economic Thinkers*. New York: Simon & Schuster, 1999.

Herman, R. Paul. *The HIP Investor: How to Do Good for Your Portfolio and the World*. Hoboken, N.J.: Wiley, 2010.

Hochschild, Adam. *Bury the Chains: Prophets and Rebels in the Fight to Free an Empire's Slaves*. New York: Houghton Mifflin, 2005.

Kramer, Mark, Marcie Parkhurst and Lalitha Vaidyanathan. *Breakthroughs in Shared Measurement and Social Impact*. Boston: FSG Social Impact Advisors, 2009 (http://fsg-impact.org/ideas/item/breakthroughs_in_measurement.html).

Light, Paul C. *The Search for Social Entrepreneurship*. Washington D.C.: Brookings Institute Press, 2008.

Machiavelli, Niccolò, *The Prince*, New York: Oxford University Press, 2008.

Madison, James. *The Federalist Paper No. 62* (http://www.constitution.org/fed/federa62.htm).

Martin, Roger, and Sally Osberg, "Social Entrepreneurship: The Case for Definition," *Stanford Social Innovation Review*, Spring, 2007.

McClelland, David. *The Achieving Society*. New York: Free Press, 1999.

Mighton, John. *The Myth of Ability: Nurturing Mathematical Talent in Every Child*. New York: Walker, 2004.

Nicholls, Alec, ed., *The Journal of Social Entrepreneurship*. London: Routledge (forthcoming).

Novogratz, Jacqueline. *The Blue Sweater: Bridging the Gap between Rich and Poor in an Interconnected World*. New York: Rodale, 2009.

O'Toole, James. *Leading Change: The Argument for Values-Based Leadership*. New York: Ballantine Books, 1996.

Palmer, Parker. *The Courage to Teach: Exploring the Inner Landscape of a Teacher's Life*. San Francisco: Jossey-Bass, 2007.

Prahalad, C.K. *The Fortune at the Bottom of the Pyramid*. New York: Wharton Business School Press, 2005.

Ray, Paul H., and Sherry R. Anderson. *The Cultural Creatives: How 50 Million People Are Changing the World*. New York: Three Rivers Press, 2001.

Sagawa, Shirley, and Deb Jospin. *The Charismatic Organization: Eight Ways to Grow a Nonprofit That Builds Buzz, Delights Donors, and Energizes Employees*. San Francisco: Jossey-Bass, 2008.

Smillie, Ian. *Freedom from Want: The Remarkable Success Story of BRAC, the Global Grassroots Organization That's Winning the Fight Against Poverty*. Sterling, VA: Kumarian Press, 2009.

Smith, Adam. *The Wealth of Nations*. New York: Oxford University Press, 2008.

Taylor, Frederick Winslow. *The Principles of Scientific Management*. New York BiblioLife, 2008.

Thomas, Lewis. *The Lives of a Cell*. Viking Adult, 1974.

De Tocqueville, Alexis. *Democracy in America*. New York: Signet Classics, 2001.

Trelstad, Brian, "Simple Measures for Social Enterprise," *Innovations*, Summer 2008 (www.mitpressjournals.org/doi/pdf/10.1162/itgg.2008.3.3.105).

Wolk, Andrew, "Advancing Social Entrepreneurship: Recommendations for Policy Makers and Government Agencies," Aspen Institute, Root Cause, 2008 (http://www.aspeninstitute.org/atf/cf/%7BDEB6F227-659B-4EC8-8F84-8DF23CA704F5%7D/nspp_AdvSocEntrp.pdf).

Wright, Robert. *Nonzero: The Logic of Human Destiny*. New York: Vintage, 2001.

Yunus, Muhammad, with Karl Weber. *Creating a World without Poverty: Social Business and the Future of Capitalism*. New York: Public Affairs, 2007.

Yunus, Muhammad. *Banker to the Poor: Micro-Lending and the Battle against World Poverty*. New York: Public Affairs, 1999.

Other recommended books and articles

Ashoka Social Entrepreneurship Series (16 DVDs), published by Ashoka's Global Academy. Available at www.ashoka.org.

Austin, James E. *The Collaboration Challenge: How Nonprofits and Businesses Succeed Through Strategic Alliances*. San Francisco: Jossey-Bass Publishers, 2000.

Bamburg, Jill. *Getting to Scale: Growing Your Business without Selling Out*. San Francisco: Berrett-Koehler Publishers, Inc., 2006.

Bhatt, Ela R. *We Are Poor but So Many: The Story of Self-Employed Women in India*. New York: Oxford University Press, 2005.

Bornstein, David. *How to Change the World: Social Entrepreneurs and the Power of New Ideas*. New York: Oxford University Press, 2004.

Bornstein, David. "So You Want to Change the World?" Hart House Lecture, University of Toronto, 2005 (http://www.davidbornstein. com).

Bornstein, David. *The Price of a Dream: The Story of the Grameen Bank*. New York: Oxford University Press, 1997.

Bronson, Po and Ashley Merryman. *Nurture Shock: New Thinking about Children*. New York: Twelve, 2009.

Clinton, Bill. *Giving: How Each of Us Can Change the World*. New York: Knopf, 2007.

Collins, Jim. *Good to Great and the Social Sectors: A Monograph to Accompany Good to Great*. New York: HarperCollins, 2005.

Conley, Chip, and Eric Friedenwald-Fishman. *Marketing That Matters: 10 Practices to Profit Your Business and Change the World*. San Francisco: Berrett-Koehler Publishers, 2006.

Counts, Alex. *Small Loans, Big Dreams: How Nobel Prize Winner Muhammad Yunus and Microfinance Are Changing the World*. New York: Wiley, 2008.

Davis, Susan M. "Social Entrepreneurship: Towards an Entrepreneurial Culture for Social and Economic Development." Abstract, Social Science Research Network (http://ssrn.com/abstract=978868).

Davis, Susan M. and Vinod Khosla, "The Architecture of Audacity: Assessing the Impact of the Microcredit Summit Campaign," *Innovations: Technology, Governance, Globalization* Winter/Spring 2007, Vol. 2, No. 1–2: 159–180. MIT Press Journals.

Davis, Susan and Fazle Hasan Abed, "Towards Cultures of Peace, Equality and Development," in *Vancouver Peace Summit, Selected Writings*, Dalai Lama Peace and Education Center, Vancouver, 2009.

Dees, J. Greg. "The Meaning of Social Entrepreneurship," 1998 (http://www.caseatduke.org/documents/dees_sedef.pdf).

Dees, J. Greg & Beth Anderson, "Framing a Theory of Social Entrepreneurship: Building on Two Schools of Practice and Thought," *Research on Social Entrepreneurship: Understanding and Contributing to an Emerging Field* (Volume 1, Number 3), Indianapolis, IN: Arnova (www.arnova.org).

Dees, J. Greg, Beth Anderson, and Jane Wei-Skillern, "Scaling Social Impact," *Stanford Social Innovation Review*, Spring 2004, pp.24-32.

Dees, J. Greg. *Strategic Tools for Social Entrepreneurs: Enhancing the Performance of Your Enterprising Nonprofit*, with co-editors Jed Emerson and Peter Economy San Francisco: Wiley, 2002.

Dees, J. Greg, "Rhetoric, Research, and Reality: Building a Solid Foundation for the Practice of Social Entrepreneurship," with Beth Battle Anderson, in Nicholls, ed., *Social Entrepreneurship: New Models of Sustainable Social Change*. New York: Oxford University Press, 2006.

Dev Appanah, S. and Sunit Shrestha. *Startup & Change the World: Guide for Young Social Entrepreneurs*, Youth Social Enterprise Initiative, 2007 (http://www.ysei.org).

Drayton, William, "The Citizen Sector Transformed" in Nicholls, ed., *Social Entrepreneurship: New Models of Sustainable Social Change*. New York: Oxford University Press, 2006.

Drayton, William, "Everyone a Changemaker: Social Entrepreneurship's Ultimate Goal," Ashoka, 2006 (http://www.ashoka.org/sites/ashoka/files/InnovationsBookletSmall.pdf).

Drucker, Peter. *Innovation and Entrepreneurship*. New York: Harper & Row, 1985.

Duggan, William. *Strategic Intuition: The Creative Spark in Human Achievement*. New York: Columbia Business School, 2007.

Easterly, William. *The White Man's Burden: Why the West's Efforts to Aid the Rest Have Done So Much Ill and So Little Good*. New York: Penguin, 2006.

Emerson, Jed and Shelia Bonini. "The Blended Value Map: Tracking the Intersects and Opportunities of Economic, Social and Environmental Value Creation," revised January 2004 (http://www.blendedvalue.org/)

Emerson, Jed, Tim Freundlich and Jim Fruchterman. "Nothing Ventured, Nothing Gained, Addressing The Critical Gaps In Risk-Taking Capital For Social Enterprise," Skoll Centre for Social Entrepreneurship, 2007 (www.benetech.org/about/downloads/Nothing VenturedFINAL.pdf).

Foster, William and Jeffrey Bradach. "Should Nonprofits Seek Profits?" *Harvard Business Review*, Feb. 2005 (www.probono.net/library/attachment.61472).

Gergen, Chris and Gregg Vanourek. *Life Entrepreneurs: Ordinary People Creating Extraordinary Lives*. San Francisco: Jossey-Bass, 2008.

Gerzon, Mark. *Leading Through Conflict: How Successful Leaders Transform Differences into Opportunities*. Boston: Harvard Business Press, 2006.

Gordon, Mary. *Roots of Empathy: Changing the World Child by Child*. Markham, ON: Thomas Allen Publishers, 2005.

Haidt, Jonathan. *The Happiness Hypothesis: Finding Modern Truth in Ancient Wisdom*. New York: Basic Books, 2005.

Hart, Stuart. *Capitalism at the Crossroads: The Unlimited Business Opportunities in Solving the World's Problems*. New York: Wharton School Publishing, 2005.

Heath, Chip and Dan Heath. *Made to Stick: Why Some Ideas Survive and Others Die*. New York: Random House, 2007.

Hubbard, R. Glenn and William Duggan. *The Aid Trap: Hard Truths About Ending Poverty*. New York: Columbia Business School Press, 2009.

Hustad, Amy and Jennifer Macauley, Martha Piper, Shirley Sagawa, Rachel Shatten, Kim Syman, Kelly Ward, *America Forward*

Briefing Book, New Profit Inc. (http://www.americaforward.org/ wp-content/documents/AmericaForwardbriefingbook_2007.pdf).

Jacobs, Jane. *Systems of Survival: A Dialogue on the Moral Foundations of Commerce and Politics*. New York: Vintage Books, 1994.

Jones, Van. *The Green Collar Economy: How One Solution Can Fix Our Two Biggest Problems*. New York: HarperCollins, 2008.

Kidder, Tracy. *Mountains Beyond Mountains: The Quest of Dr. Paul Farmer, a Man Who Would Cure the World*. New York: Random House, 2004.

Kielburger, Craig and Marc Kielburger. *Me to We: Finding Meaning in a Material World*. New York: Fireside, 2005.

Kincade, Sheila and Christina Macy. *Our Time is Now: Young People Changing the World*. Boston: Pearson Foundation, 2005.

Kopp, Wendy. *One Day All Children...: The Unlikely Triumph Of Teach For America And What I Learned Along The Way*. New York: Public Affairs, 2003.

Krebs, Betsy and Paul Pitcoff. *Beyond the Foster Care System: The Future for Teens*. Piscataway: Rutgers University Press, 2006.

Kristof, Nicholas D. and Sheryl WuDunn. *Half the Sky: Turning Oppression into Opportunity for Women Worldwide*. New York: Knopf, 2009.

Lessing, Doris. *Prisons We Choose to Live Inside*. New York: Harper Perennial, 1987.

Maathai, Wangari. *Unbowed: A Memoir*. New York: Knopf, 2006.

Maathai, Wangari. *The Challenge for Africa*. New York: Pantheon, 2009.

Mair, Johanna, Jeffrey Robinson, and Kai Hockerts. *Social Entrepreneurship*. New York: Palgrave, 2006.

Mathews, Jay. *Work Hard, Be Nice: How Two Inspired Teachers Created the Most Promising Schools in America*. New York: Algonquin Paperbacks, 2009.

McGray, Douglas. "The Instigator," *The New Yorker*, May 11, 2009, p. 66.

Murray, Anne Firth. *Paradigm Found: Leading and Managing for Positive Change*. Novato, CA: New World Library, 2006.

Nicholls, Alex, ed., *Social Entrepreneurship: New Models of Sustainable Social Change*. New York: Oxford University Press, 2006.

Nunn, Michele, ed., *Be the Change: Change the World, Change Yourself*. Atlanta: Hundreds of Heads Books, 2006.

Overholser, George. "Nonprofit Growth Capital, Part One, Building Is Not Buying," Nonprofit Finance Fund (http://www.nonprofitfinancefund.org/docs/Building%20is%20Not%20Buying.pdf).

Overholser, George, "Patient Capital: The Next Step Forward?" Nonprofit Finance Fund (www.nonprofitfinancefund.org/docs/Patient%20 Capital%20Final.pdf).

Palmer, Parker. *Let Your Life Speak: Listening for the Voice of Vocation*. San Francisco: Jossey-Bass, 1999.

Patel, Eboo. *Acts of Faith: The Story of an American Muslim, the Struggle for the Soul of a Generation*. New York: Beacon Press, 2007.

Patterson, Kerry, et al. *Influencer: The Power to Change Anything*. New York: McGraw-Hill, 2007.

Polak, Paul. *Out of Poverty: What Works When Traditional Approaches Fail.* San Francisco, Berrett Koehler, 2008.

Pressman, Jeffrey L., and Aaron Wildavsky. *Implementation.* Berkeley: University of California Press, 1984.

Pressman, Steven. *The War of Art: Break Through the Blocks and Win Your Inner Creative Battles.* New York: Grand Central Publishing, 2003.

Quinn, Robert E. *Change the World: How Ordinary People Can Accomplish Extraordinary Results.* San Francisco: Jossey-Bass, 2000.

Roberts, Sam. *A Kind of Genius: Herb Sturz and Society's Toughest Problems.* New York: Public Affairs, 2009.

Robinson, Jeffrey, Johanna Mair, and Kai Hockerts, editors. *International Perspectives on Social Entrepreneurship,* New York: Palgrave Macmillan, 2009.

Schorr, Lisbeth. *Common Purpose: Strengthening Families and Neighborhoods to Rebuild America.* New York: Anchor Books 1998.

Seabrook, John. "Don't Shoot," *The New Yorker,* June 22, 2009, p. 32.

Shapiro, Joseph P. *No Pity: People with Disabilities Forging a New Civil Rights Movement.* New York: Times Books, 1993.

Shields, Sandra, and David Campion. *The Company of Others: Stories of Belonging.* Vancouver: Arsenal Pulp Press/PLAN Institute, 2005.

Sieber, Sam. *Fatal Remedies: The Ironies of Social Intervention.* New York: Plenum Press, 1981.

Snibbe, Alana Conner, "Drowning in Data," *Stanford Social Innovation Review,* Fall 2006, pp. 39–45.

Stevens, Susan Kenny. *Nonprofit Lifecycles: Stage-based Wisdom for Nonprofit Capacity.* Long Lake: MN, Stagewise Enterprises, Inc., 2003.

Tough, Paul. *Whatever it Takes: Geoffrey Canada's Quest to Change Harlem and America.* New York: Houghton Mifflin Harcourt, 2008.

Tracey, Paul and Owen Jarvis, "An Enterprising Failure: Why a Promising Social Franchise Collapsed," *Stanford Social Innovation Review,* Spring 2006, pp. 66–70 (www.ssireview.org/pdf/2006SP_casestudy_Tracey_Jarvis.pdf).

Weiser, John, Michele Kahane, Steve Rochlin, and Jessica Landis. *Untapped: Creating Value in Underserved Markets.* San Francisco: Berrett-Koehler Publishers, 2006.

Wei-Skillern, Jane C., et al. *Entrepreneurship in the Social Sector.* Thousand Oaks: Sage Publications, 2007.

Westley, Frances, Brenda Zimmerman, and Michael Patton. *Getting to Maybe: How the World Is Changed.* Toronto: Vintage Canada, 2007.

Wood, John. *Leaving Microsoft to Change the World: An Entrepreneur's Odyssey to Educate the World's Children.* New York: Harper Business, 2006.

INDEX

CPSIA information can be obtained at www.ICGtesting.com
Printed in the USA
BVOW02*0927290713

327140BV00003B/19/P

9 780195 396348